T0294404

All Rise!

The Libertarian Way
With Judge Jim Gray

Judge James P. Gray (ret.)

All Rise!
The Libertarian Way
With Judge Jim Gray

With a Preface by
Congressman Tom Campbell

GAUDIUM

Gaudium Publishing

Las Vegas ◊ Oxford ◊ Palm Beach

Published in the United States of America by
Histria Books, a division of Histria LLC
7181 N. Hualapai Way
Las Vegas, NV 89166 USA
HistriaBooks.com

Gaudium Publishing is an imprint of Histria Books. Titles published under the imprints of Histria Books are distributed worldwide.

Library of Congress Control Number: 2020943083

ISBN 978-1-59211-080-3 (hardcover)
ISBN 978-1-59211-092-6 (softbound)

Table of Contents

Preface
by Congressman Tom Campbell

Judge Jim Gray is a man of principle. He has thought long and deeply about what principles should govern human behavior. In his public life, his own actions and positions have adhered to those principles. The result is the approach to public policy that he sets forth in this book.

Judge Gray has specific proposals for almost all of our society's challenges. Even more importantly, he illustrates how those proposals follow from principle, so that one has a guide to resolving problems to come, which might be only dimly seen today. The principle is individual liberty married to responsibility. If a public policy proposal increases individual liberty, we should favor it, provided no one else is specifically hurt. It is amazing how many of today's seemingly intractable problems yield solutions under that principle.

Today, we are shocked by the behavior of foreign governments. Judge Gray's principle says let the people of those countries emulate us, or not, as they wish and as they are able. What should we not do? Bomb them into agreement with us.

The two major parties have outlived their usefulness. It's no surprise that Judge Gray's affinity for the individual leaves little admiration for the orthodoxy demanded of candidates running under the banners of the two major parties today. There was a time, when both he and I were starting in public life, that the two major parties tolerated a healthy degree of internal debate. Today, however, complete adherence to policies prescribed by party chieftains is demanded. For example, no tax can ever be supported by a Republican candidate, even if a carbon tax is a more efficient way to curb greenhouse gases than the heavy-handed present approach of government set emission limits. No school voucher program can be defended by a Democratic candidate, even though school choice empowers parents of lower income with an alternative to their child's failing school. Judge Gray joined the Libertarian Party because it came closest to his ideal of individual liberty. I formed a new party dedicated to encouraging fact-based decisions on all matters of public policy. Neither of us take well to being ordered what to believe.

Judge Gray made his inaugural foray into public policy when in April of 1992, as a sitting judge, uniquely among all judicial officers in our country, he condemned America's drug laws. He asked what business is it of the government what one chooses to put into one's own body? We all agree we should prevent driving a car while high or giving drugs to minors. Otherwise, however, the pathologies of drug use that affect others are largely not due to the drug itself, but to the very making of the drug illegal.

Criminals sell the illegal drugs, make exorbitant profits because they are illegal, and bribe officials to allow them to continue — across the world. Had Judge Gray's prescription been followed, all profit would be eliminated from illegal drugs and the problem would solve itself. Without pushers, drug use would drop precipitously. The evidence of Portugal, Netherlands and Switzerland demonstrates that.

In America, one of the greatest reasons for the racial divide in persons put in jail are the drug laws. Some prosecutors speak of getting someone "into the system" by prosecuting that person for drug possession with intent to sell — and ever thereafter that person acts only with the permission of government through the courts, probation officers, and too often, subsequent prosecutors.

The force of government is felt most keenly by those marginalized, often on racial lines. Lower the force of government, and the disparate impact upon the marginalized will diminish.

This is an example of where Judge Gray's foresighted principles could have averted problems not yet seen at the time he announced them. Had Judge Gray's advice to lighten up government police presence been followed, our country might have been spared the recent horrible events of killing by police officers and the social unrest that has followed.

Another aspect of Judge Gray's beneficial take on the drug wars is in foreign policy. Judge Gray's advice would have saved America's allies the development of drug production in their own countries (as well as saving us expenses in border security and foreign aid). Judge Gray and I saw this problem alike. When additional money was proposed for Colombia to eradicate coca leaf production, I was a Member of the U.S. Congress. I voted no and predicted that once Colombia knew its receipt of U.S. aid was keyed to fighting the drug war, the war would never end. It hasn't.

Judge Gray does see a role for government. In our free market economy, it is essential for government to guarantee a competitive marketplace, allowing individuals to make choices from among the goods and services that are offered. Pharmaceutical companies must not be permitted to drive a competitor out of the market. All should then be allowed to compete. Since we can't know the safety of drugs on our own, the government should decide whether a particular therapy is likely to do harm. Those risks should be made plain to the consumer. Thereafter, the consumer's choice should govern. The U.S. government demands more: that a drug must be proven effective as well as safe. Whether or not a drug is effective should be left to the consumer, advised as she or he wishes by her or his doctor. That one change in the law would both lower the cost of pharmaceuticals and save lives.

Judge Gray not only thinks from principle, he acts from principle and has done so all his adult life. As a California trial judge, his innovations in drug courts, veterans' courts, and juvenile peer panels lessened the heavy press of government and reinforced the responsibility of the individual. Lives were rescued because of Judge Gray. Dignity was restored to individuals because Judge Gray treated criminal defendants as individuals, and their trajectories were forever altered for the better. He did the same in the Peace Corps, giving two years of his life to the people of Costa Rica to improve their learning, health, and futures. He has taken care of others because of the inherent worth of each person.

Judge Gray is his brother's keeper, and his example compels each of us to be so as well. If we are our brother's keeper, there is a less perceived need for Big Brother to take on that function.

Knowing that Judge Gray actually implemented many of the ideas put forward in this book, the reader should be reassured that the policy suggestions are both practical and principled. Judge Gray's test for success is not the beauty of theory, but whether people are better off for the practice of the policy. Because his belief in individual liberty, married to responsibility, is principled, we can extrapolate his advice to problems not yet imagined.

This book is a thoughtful review of many of today's problems, demonstrating that their solutions are not intractable at all. More importantly, it is also an invocation to champion the highest attribute of the human being: the liberty of an individual. To maximize that virtue is to exercise what distinguishes our modern society from all that have gone before it, and to vindicate today what has distinguished America among nations. We are the freest people the world has ever seen. Judge Gray has helped our country achieve that reality in the past; his principles will guide us to continue to do so in the future.

Introduction

Welcome to a rather full discussion of my views of the Libertarian philosophy and how, when put into operation, it would change our world in so many important ways — and all for the better! Along the way, I also give various illustrative examples of those results by citing various experiences from my own life. A fair amount of what follows is taken from my prior writings, so I acknowledge that some points are made more than once. But I repeated them because I feel that they are important and worth your continued thought. And the title of this book is the same as my weekly podcast on the Variety Channel of www.VoiceAmerica.com, with the play on words that bailiffs normally cry out when a judge first takes the bench. But the premise of both this book and the podcast is that if we employ Libertarian values and approaches, we will "All Rise" together.

So, as you will see, we discuss many issues from a Libertarian perspective in the eleven chapters that follow, including our nation's roots, Justice in our political system as it was first established and then as it has evolved, Over-Incarceration, Economics, Healthcare, Education, how we often both hinder and help our Children, War, Immigration, Religion and our country's failed policy of Drug Prohibition.

Of course, no one in this world "has all of the answers," and that most certainly includes me. But I do firmly believe that we should be able to *discuss* virtually anything. So please sit back with me and ponder how our world would be so much better with governments that would lead with and employ these Libertarian principles! For more information, please visit www.JudgeJimGray.com, and thank you for your interest!

Chapter 1

Liberty Is In Our Genes

In 1620, the Mayflower departed from the shores of England, a merchant ship with one-hundred-and-two Pilgrims on board seeking a new life in the New World. Once they reached the shores of Cape Cod, they adopted what could be seen as a socialist or even communist system of living, principled in the concept of "From everyone according to their abilities, to everyone according to their needs." Crops were raised communally and shared with people in accordance with their needs. But this utopian vision was so devastating in practice that many people actually starved during the first winter. As such, it was clear that an operational overhaul was necessary. So the Pilgrims switched to a system where people could live in Liberty from as much government intrusion as possible, and also profit from their own industry and labors. And thereafter, they thrived.

The colonies, over time, adapted to that new way of doing things. In fact, by the time that the 55 delegates met at the 1787 Constitutional Convention that view was so engrained that, although they bickered, debated and even fought about many things, there was one singular point they all agreed upon: the most important function of government is to protect our freedoms and liberties from the encroachment of government. (The second most important was keeping us safe.) Unfortunately, that principle has gotten lost in much of American politics today, but it still runs through the blood and veins of the Libertarian Party.

Margaret Thatcher once famously observed that "The trouble with socialism is that eventually you run out of other people's money." Unfortunately, the situation in our country today is worse than that. Despite over $24 Trillion and counting in public debt, politicians are still promising voters something for nothing. This simply must stop. It is a poison for everybody, and particularly our young people! Instead of falling for these promises, we must unite under a singular cause, which is our great nation's founding principle: Liberty.

As stated above, Liberty is in our country's DNA. Our Declaration of Independence focuses on "Life, Liberty and the Pursuit of Happiness," our Constitution was ordained, among other things, to "Secure the Blessings of Liberty to ourselves and our Posterity," and the Pledge of Allegiance to our country's flag ends with the phrase "with Liberty and Justice for All." But what exactly is Liberty? A dictionary will tell you that Liberty is the state of being free in a society. But free from what? Free from oppressive restrictions thrust upon our lives, political views, and behaviors by authority. But what authority would do such a thing? The government.

But to be free, to be in a state of Liberty, is a double-edged sword. In a state of Liberty, you can make your own choices. There are no external obstacles barring you, as an adult, from living your life as you choose, as long as that does not wrongly affect the ability of other adults to do the same. But that's just one edge of the sword. The other edge holds you responsible for your own self-determination, your destiny, and your interests. Thus Liberty is one prong of a two-pronged bargain: enjoy your state of freedom but take seriously the responsibilities that come with it.

There's a pervasive myth around Liberty that it's a "no holds barred, anything goes" philosophy. The truth is that Liberty is far from such an egalitarian vision. Of course, we need government, if only for the purposes set forth in Article 1, Section 8 of the Constitution (which delegates specific powers to Congress). We need a military, national police, and a judiciary to enforce laws that protect our rights, persons, and property from wrongful assaults and takings by others. We need the means to enforce contracts, warranties, child-labor laws, safety in the workplace and anti-trust so that we can live under the Rule of Law together. This Liberty approach has done us well as long as it has been employed. Liberty involves responsibility at every level of society, including personal, group, corporate, and governmental.

Many people, however, subconsciously shy away from Liberty because it brings choices and accountability for the consequences of the choices they make. When I was the social chairman for our Delta Tau Delta fraternity at UCLA, I was organizing the Holiday Party at a local hotel. But I made a mistake and left it up to the members to decide whether we would have champagne or mixed drinks at the party. Forty-five minutes later, after much discussion and disagreement, the members, in a close election, voted for champagne. But, I found this left many of the members upset. So when I organized the Spring party, I simply announced that we would have mixed drinks and that it was going to be great. As a result, I saved lots of time, and everyone was happy. Sometimes people prefer to have others make decisions for them, as long as the decisionmaker appears confident. Of course, I had no nefarious intentions and my ability to wield power was limited to organizing a Spring party for my fraternity. But the government, on the other hand, has unbelievable power. The more we are sold a narrative of fear, the more docile we become. Let me explain.

Michael Baroni, a former president of the Orange County Bar Association who introduced me before I received the Lifetime Achievement Award from that wonderful organization, once told me about a popular Russian parable. "This is how to catch wild pigs," he began. "You find a place in the woods and put out some food. The pigs, once they find it, will return every day to eat the free food. Then, once the pigs have acclimated to their new daily habit, put a fence down on one side of the place where they come to eat. Once they have acclimated to the fence, they'll eat the food again, which is when you then put up the other side of the fence. Continue doing this until you've installed four sides of fence and then finish it off with a gate. The wild pigs will come through that gate to eat more food, after which you close the gate, and you've caught the whole herd!" That parable is an astute metaphor to what happens in government. Lofty promises and temporary handouts lure people in, only to realize later that they have lost their liberties. Thus, in that regard, relying upon the government is a trap.

So Liberty, indeed, can be a scary thing. But that isn't a strong enough argument to toss it aside. In 2003, the notorious founder of gonzo journalism, Hunter S. Thompson, wrote: "We are turning into a nation of whimpering slaves to Fear — fear of war, fear of poverty, fear of random terrorism, fear of getting down-sized or fired because of the plunging economy, fear of getting evicted for bad debts, or suddenly getting locked up in a military detention camp on vague charges of being a Terrorist sympathizer. These things have already happened to millions of patriotic law-abiding American citizens, and it will happen to many more." So we owe it to ourselves, our ancestors, and our Founders to be vigilant!

One of my first recollections of being afraid was when I was about three years old. My parents had purchased a black cat costume for me to wear for Halloween, complete with a long tail. But I scared myself so much that I could only be convinced to go to our neighboring two houses. Then that was enough.

Similarly, big government trades on keeping us in fear as a justification for encroaching upon our Liberty. Be truthful with yourself: did it really have an impact on you when Edward Snowden revealed that our government routinely was accessing our bank accounts and cell phone information? What would our Founders say about those encroachments on our Liberty? What would they say about us tolerating them? If we continue to react to what we fear, America's true heyday may never come to fruition. But if we embrace our fears and accept them as an opportunity for societal growth, we're on a better path. Thus the three-year-old me would have had a fuller trick-or-treat candy bag. That's the path I envision for America, and a path the earliest settlers on this great continent once walked.

Henry Ford once said that any people who think they can prosper by relying upon assistance from the government should talk to the American Indian. Native Americans have the highest poverty rate of any minority group in our country. That comes largely as a result of having been controlled by the federal government since the early 1800s. Their lands are held in "trust" for them by the Bureau of Indian Affairs, or BIA (which most Native Americans refer to as "Bossing Indians Around"), which has a budget of $3 billion per year. The Bureau of Indian Education spends $850 million of that money per year on educating 42,000 students, which comes out to more than $20,000 per student per year — while the national average is about $12,500 per student. So money is not the problem. Those two government agencies, by the way, have 9,000 employees, which pencils out to about one bureaucrat for every 111 Native Americans still on the reservations. What's the answer? End the trust system and government supervision. It's time to bring in Liberty! As an analogy, Irish immigrants had the stereotypical reputation of indulging in too much alcohol. So should we have had a Bureau of Irish Affairs? Obviously not. When people are held responsible for the decisions they make, they are much more likely to make good decisions. (It certainly worked for the Irish Americans!)

So what is so good about the Free Enterprise System? It directly results in a system where most people end up working and doing things that they do best. They can profit from those efforts by buying and selling with others. In other words, it mostly results in what John Stossel calls a "Double Thank You Moment." That means, for example, that manufacturers of washing machines, since they have lots of them, value a customer's cash more than the machine itself. But the purchasers, obviously, places greater value on the washing machine than on the amount of money they will pay. So, when the deal is done, both the customers and the manufacturer say "thank you" to one another. Each one of them wins. Within a free society, that happens countless times per day in all sectors of life.

Dr. Milton Friedman, one of my true heroes and the Nobel Prize winning economist who I will quote quite often in the pages to come, was deeply skeptical of government reliance as well. He once stated that no modern society has ever raised itself out of poverty except through a system based upon free enterprise and private property rights. Of course, that doesn't mean that we should not voluntarily provide a Safety Net for those people who are truly in need. I was in the Peace Corps: I care about people. Though we have no legal obligation to support anybody, I do believe a safety net for our people is crucial. My proposal would combine a Federal Graduated Income Flat Tax with a system of government stipends proposed by Milton Friedman. The flat tax means, with these numbers used only for illustration, that no one will pay any federal income taxes on the first $30,000 of earnings — not you, me, or even Bill Gates. But all differentiations between earned and interest income and capital gains would be dissolved. Then for every dollar earned between $30,001 and $100,000, each person would pay 8 cents to the government, with no deductions involved! For those fortunate enough to earn between $100,001 and $500,000 in a year, they would pay 12 cents on those dollars, and those blessed to make above $500,000 per year would pay 20 cents for those dollars. End of discussion.

So now, what about the poor? Everyone in our country who is 18 years of age or older and is either a citizen or a green card holder who earns no money would receive a stipend from the federal government of $15,000 a year, probably broken into monthly payments of $1,250. But for every dollar they earned between zero and $30,000, they would lose 50 cents of their stipend. Thus, of critical importance, everyone would always have a financial incentive to earn the extra dollar — which is fundamentally missing in today's welfare system!

Parenthetically, if you paid attention to the Democratic Primaries in late 2019, Andrew Yang's proposal for a Universal Basic Income is a more egalitarian solution—offering $1,000 per month for every taxpaying American regardless of income levels. My approach does away with that bureaucracy and many needless payments. As such,

$30,000 would be the break-even point where people would receive no stipends but pay no taxes. Then we eliminate all other forms of welfare, except for those people with truly special needs. Although this certainly is an imperfect approach, this proposed system would be far more efficient, fair, and transparent than what we are doing today. It would not only make the amount of taxes we pay abundantly clear; it would also make it clear when politicians were raising (or, imagine that, lowering) our taxes!

A truly added plus would be that this proposed system would come close to resolving the homeless problem on an institutional basis. How is that? Today's responses mostly come about when politicians feel some political heat, which often results in large amounts of public money being spent on things like putting up the homeless in motels for a few months. Then they turn to other "pressing needs," while after those few months, the homeless problems go on as before. But if the homeless had the equivalent of an ATM account that automatically had $1,250 in it each month, the Free Enterprise System would quickly respond by establishing fairly inexpensive room and board facilities, which would still leave the homeless with some funds to purchase clothing and to cover other everyday necessities. (Of course, many of the homeless are mentally ill or have a dependence upon mind-altering drugs. But if they need a conservatorship or drug treatment, those are separate issues that can and should be addressed by the local communities and governments.)

Actually, I wasn't born a Libertarian. I grew up with Republican parents and, when I turned 21, I registered as a Republican as well. And I wasn't just an idle voter either, I joined the Finance Committee of the Republican Party in our county. In addition, I also took a leave of absence from the court to run for Congress in the 1998 Republican primary election against former Congressman Robert Dornan. I lost to Dornan, and he eventually lost again to Democratic Congresswoman Loretta Sanchez in the general election. But the moment I knew my values no longer aligned with the party in which I claimed membership was when President George W. Bush signed into law the so-called Patriot Act on October 26, 2001. Designed to play upon obvious public fears after the tragedies of September 11, 2001, I could not support a party that would condone, much less assist, this direct and frontal attack upon our freedoms and liberties. I remember it well; it took me all of 13 seconds to decide that I really am a Libertarian, and I will be a Libertarian for life. As the Russian parable suggests, lofty promises and temporary handouts lure people in, only to realize later that they have lost their liberties. And here we are, nearly two decades after the passage of the so-called Patriot Act, yet many of its provisions are continually renewed with no promises fulfilled. Do you think that the government will ever announce that the so-called War on Terror will be over? Not a chance! Benjamin Franklin once famously said that any people who would give up a little liberty for a little more security deserve neither. I agree with Dr. Franklin.

In 2012, I ran for Vice President as a Libertarian alongside Gary Johnson, and eight years before that, I ran as a Libertarian for a seat in the United States Senate. Each time, I held firmly to my Libertarian principles and continued to be motivated by the realization I had as a senior in high school, which was that one of the worst things that could ever happen to a person is to be on their death bed looking back over their lives and lamenting that "I wish I would have," or "I wish I would not have." I have tried not to let that happen to me. So, I joined the Peace Corps, climbed Mt. Whitney, traveled to Turkey, and even ran for the nomination of the Libertarian Party for President in 2020.

Bluntly speaking, however, there is one big mistake that Libertarians have made — for decades! And that is that we have allowed other people to label us. In fact, if you arbitrarily put a net over a group of one hundred people and ask them what Libertarians stand for, almost all of them would respond with something along the lines of no government at all, anarchy, "greed is good," everyone should use drugs, totally open borders, or that we are the party of the "survival of the fittest." But that's simply not the case. We are a Party of Principle, and a party that aims to preserve your ability to live your life as you wish. But what we propose actually works!

I also go beyond that because I further believe that the Libertarian Party is the only political party in the mainstream of American political thought today. How so? Because we are the only ones who do not wish to profit by being involved in government. That is simply not true with any other political party. They all give taxpayer money to their favorite recipients, thus, in large part, buying the recipients' votes with our tax money, just like they bail out some businesses and not others. For example, are you aware that the Secretary of the Department of the Treasury in response to the OVID-19 crisis was voted by Congress to have a $550 billion slush fund to hand out to whichever businesses he chose? So, for example, the Kennedy Center in Washington DC was given more than $20 million. Why, someone audaciously asked? Because the Center was injured by being forced to close its doors. Of course it was, but what about all of the other theaters in the country who were similarly hurt? Nothing. (Although, as you probably also heard, when faced with this reality, the Kennedy Center returned the money.) In other words, when governments under today's political parties are not being arbitrary, they are playing favorites. Not so with Libertarians.

So my quest, and the quest of this book, is to help propel the Libertarian Party into the conscious mainstream of American political thought. America's Presidential playing field, however, poses an irony to the Libertarian platform. The system is set up to give you two choices: Democrat or Republican. Then, what do we call the rest of us in most political polls? A category lazily labeled "Other?" No. We are Libertarians, and we're ready to put up a good fight despite an electoral system that's rigged against us. What do I mean, rigged? Well, the Presidential Debates are a good starting point to understanding how our political processes have been hijacked by those at the top who are fearful of true competition. Like I said earlier, if we allow the politics of fear to persist, the best version of the United States will remain untapped, and unable to flourish.

When is the last time you've seen a candidate on the debate stage that isn't a member of one of the two dominant parties? There was once a time when debates were run differently. Under the leadership of the League of Women Voters, candidates from any political party that was on the ballot in enough states technically to win the presidential election were invited to participate. Tragically for our country, the League was eventually frozen out of the process by high-ranking Republican and Democratic Commission members. But the League didn't go quietly, because it left with the public statement that "We will not be a part of the hoodwinking of America!" Nevertheless, the debates, under the complete control of these two parties, have kept America hoodwinked ever since that time.

Candidates since that time have only been invited on the stage if they showed fifteen percent ratings in five national polls — and those polls aren't even named until after the invitations are issued! In addition, they even control aspects of operating debates by choosing moderators, topics to be discussed by the candidates, and how long candidates will have to answer the questions.

Liberty demands that this fraud on the voters be reversed. Not only do debates give legitimacy and viability to candidates who participate, but they also largely control the issues that are presented to the public. At a very minimum, if a third party candidate were on the stage, all candidates would be required to talk about issues that otherwise would not be discussed, such as the deficit, never-ending wars, the verifiable fact that too many of our government schools are failing our children, the rising costs of medical care under the control of governments, and many more. Comfortable mainstream party candidates won't take positions until they are forced to, and real competition is the only way for that to occur.

Historically, third parties have played a critical role in American politics in two distinct ways. First, third parties have actually managed to rise to become a main party, although the last time that happened was when the Republicans took over the Whig Party in the late 1850s. Second, third parties have voiced new ideas that have resonated with voters, resulting in the assimilation of those ideas into mainstream political thought. It is this new blood that keeps the American political process vibrant, responsive, and productive.

What do we do when we're battling in a system that's mostly weighted against third-party voices? Beyond the excessive gatekeeping of the Presidential debates, the gerrymandering of congressional districts by the two main parties has kept many political races non-competitive. Political pollsters don't include the names of third-party candidates because their campaigns are not covered by the media and, therefore, remain a shadow to the public. So why doesn't the media cover third party campaigns? Because they do not receive good polling numbers. Needless to say, it's a vicious cycle that makes it nearly impossible for third-party candidates to break out of obscurity — unless they are able to self-finance their campaign, as Ross Perot did.

So how do we break this cycle? Let's start with the debates. Allow every candidate that is on even one statewide ballot to participate, in some fashion, in these very public debates. Just by allowing each one to make a three-minute statement at the beginning of each debate would allow voters to hear and consider each candidate's most important issues first-hand. Third-party candidates have much to add to the free flow of ideas. But when their voices are stifled, democracy loses.

One day I was driving with my children, then aged seven, seven, and four, down a rural highway when we passed by a strawberry field. This one had sheets of plastic over it, which, I believe, reduce weeds, keep moisture in the ground, and keep the fruit cleaner. I pointed out the field to my children and said, "Look kids! That's where they raise plastic." My children responded, "Oh really, Daddy? Really?" I did not respond. But five or so miles later one of my children said, "Oh, come on Dad. That's not where they raise plastic."

That was one of my triumphs in parenting. I wanted to teach my children to challenge the source of all information, even when they are young and the source is their father. That's difficult to do because children (for all-to-short a time) tend to view their parents as all-knowing Gods. But instilling a healthy sense of curiosity and skepticism early in life is invaluable. Even if some of us learn to question what we're told later in life, those who challenge the status quo are springboards of change. I was a trial court judge for 25 years. One of the numerous things I learned is that the words "silent" and "listen" have the exact same letters in them. You learn to assess credibility from who is providing the information, you weigh the strength of the information, and then you make a decision. All voters should put themselves in that same position.

When I was in my second year of law school, just before I was sent on my Midshipman cruise to the waters of Vietnam in the summer of 1970, I wrote a poem entitled "Cast A Glance Around You" that echoes the idea of non-complacency and constructive curiosity. Here I pass it on to you:

Cast a glance around you,
Look on either side;
Vitality surrounds one
Who hastens not to hide.

The love of stars and butterflies,
The throbbing of the sea;
Some awesome parts of outer worlds,
Some inner part of me.

To sing a song to Penny Lane
With spirit strong and free;
To know that life is all there is
And there is no guarantee.

To walk with bare feet on the grass
To let the soul lift high;
To scale some rocky mountain pass
To live until you die.

Cast a glance around you
And look on either side;
Perhaps 'tis best to swim upstream
Than drift gently with the tide.

And I think I have, in many ways, been swimming upstream ever since. Dare I ask you to cast a glance around you? Look on either side. Upon closer inspection, you may exclaim as my son did many years ago, "Oh come on!" What's going on in Washington? What's going on with America? What "greater purpose" warrants these growing threats to Liberty?

Rules remain unchanged when unchallenged. Third parties across the country have a great ability and even duty to challenge the current election process and demand a public perform. Against these odds, I firmly hold that America deserves a sane, principled alternative to the politics of fear, division, tribalism, and polarization. There is a better way, built on respecting the fundamental rights of every person. Justice and prosperity, the Rule of Law, and limited government stand central to the Libertarian platform. The Libertarian Party is that much-needed alternative. We can stop endless wars, remove unjust and overly-intrusive government from our lives, abolish the so-called War on Drugs, reduce the deficits that are bound severely to harm our children, and right the rampant wrongs in our broken criminal justice system. We can restore fairness and stability to our economic lives through free and open markets.

Imagine a White House that promises to restore a sense of humility and responsibility, leadership with a four-pillared foundation of integrity, principles, honesty, and transparency. Imagine a government that respects the duties and limits of our offices, and always does the utmost to preserve, protect, and defend the individual rights of everyone. That is the Libertarian promise. We propose nothing more than the right to live your own life as you see fit, along with respect for the rights of others to do the same.

Although I understand that no one speaks for the Libertarian Party, it is fair to say once more that, unlike the Democrats and Republicans, Libertarians are not special interest driven. It is a grassroots movement that relies upon individuals who believe in the principles of freedom and who expect no favors from government in return. As such, the Libertarian Party works for the people and their rights, property, safety, and well-being, which, as a result, our approach would benefit virtually everyone in the country and, in many cases, the world. Accordingly, the Libertarian Movement today furnishes a much-needed Beacon of Hope for America.

This approach also takes into account the not-famous-enough comment from economist writer Thomas Sowell, who said: "The first lesson of economics is scarcity: there is never enough of anything to fully satisfy all those who want it. (But) the first lesson of politics is to disregard the first lesson of economics." Of course, goods and services in the real world are not free, so someone must pay for them. That is why in a Libertarian government no programs, acquisitions or other spending would be authorized unless that same authorization also would expressly designate where the money would come from to pay for them. So those are at least partial reasons for the failure of many Libertarians to be elected: because they address the first lesson of economics, while most voters remain enchanted by the first lesson of politics.

Milton Friedman once posed the question that if people believe that government will come forward and bring prosperity for all, why have we not yet seen those "Angels in Government" produce those wonderful results? Thomas Sowell also once stated, "It is hard to imagine a more stupid or more dangerous way of making decisions than by putting those decisions in the hands of people who pay no price for being wrong." Of course, this simply emphasizes the fact that there is an enormous difference between a government of stated good intentions, and a government that actually produces positive results.

Obviously, if someone in the business world makes a bad decision, there is a price to be paid. However, it is a commonly understood maxim in politics that reality is irrelevant. The only thing that matters is the voters' perception of reality. Consequently, to get a good decision, we should impose the costs of a bad decision upon the decision-maker. This can be done most effectively by having more decisions made under the rigors of the Liberty and responsibility of the marketplace, which would have fewer decisions made by those in government. Examples of this are seen in the areas of education, medical care, and even in the leasing of grazing lands. In all of these areas, the government and its bureaucrats promise good results but pay no price for poor or even bad decisions.

Many years ago, we had a Holiday Party for the entire court staff at the ballroom of a local hotel. At the end of the lunch, the presiding judge, as Master of Ceremonies, asked all clerks to stand up, where they were greeted with applause, and then all of the bailiffs, etc. But when he asked all of the Admin staff to stand, to my shock, about one-third of everyone present stood up. The next week I saw our presiding judge, called that fact to his attention, and asked what all of those people did. "It beats the hell out of me" was his response. And that was my first real glimpse into bureaucracy. They really didn't help me try my cases; they mostly shuffled papers. As I have come to see,

"Big Government is really good and effective at one thing, and that is increasing the size, power, and cost of Big Government."

Of course, bureaucracy has its place, but it can often be suffocating. It provides refuge for unnecessary inefficiency. A few years ago, I was flying on American Airlines from Orange County, California to Orlando so that I could attend the Libertarian Convention. The plane was scheduled to board at 6:15 a.m., but at 6:25 we were notified that one of the flight attendants had called in sick. Even though a substitute attendant, who lived just a few minutes away, had been contacted and was on her way, we still couldn't board until she arrived. When I asked the supervisor why we couldn't board while awaiting her arrival, I was told that it was against the rules. When I suggested she assert some leadership under these circumstances and create an exception, she responded by saying that she would be fired on the spot if she did that.

Naturally, air travel involves many issues concerning safety and prudence. However, shouldn't the answer be to employ intelligent and experienced supervisors, and then give them the Liberty to exercise discretion within their field of expertise? This is yet one more example of the many times we as a society allow bureaucratic rules to impede a more efficient and consumer-friendly result.

Libertarians do not want a system of "anything goes." Conversely, a Libertarian society where contracts and warranties are enforced provides for accountability and personal responsibility at all levels of society — individual, group, corporate, and governmental. For example, the Libertarian agenda of transforming today's government-controlled health care industry back to one that is market-driven and market-regulated will result in an explosion in medical innovation, treatments, and cures, as well as reduced costs.

And since we all are at risk of potentially any human disease, these innovations will result in greater chances for longer and healthier lives for all of us. And the same results will be seen in almost all other aspects of our lives as well.

Accordingly, under a Libertarian approach, people in general would come out ahead, and special interests and bloated governments would lose much of their power and control. Of course, life is complicated and changes always affect lots of people in many ways. So we should always be thoughtful. But the following are statements of some Libertarian principles.

Generally, Libertarians would categorize themselves as being financially responsible and socially accepting. Thus, the statement: "You are free to live your life the way you choose as long as you don't wrongly hurt other people or take their stuff" is frequently used to explain our views.

Thomas Jefferson, a prototypical Libertarian, once asserted that "I don't care if you worship one God, twenty gods or no god: It doesn't pick my pocket and it doesn't break my leg." In other words, as stated above, "Live and let live." But that philosophy does not function without a strong system of justice, which serves at least four important functions. First, it must protect us from each other (You can't wrongly break my leg). Second, it must protect our property (Or pick my pocket). Third, it must enforce our voluntary legal promises (i.e. contracts) and warranties. Fourth, it must enforce reasonable regulations that truly promote and protect the general health, safety, and welfare of the people.

Liberty is to be stressed, but where government is involved, it should strive for a world in which people are held responsible for their own behavior and are also able to profit from their own industry. Why? As Dr. Milton Friedman said, "Incentives matter." It is a universal truth that people respond to incentives. One of my disappointments as a child can be attributed to my personal miscalculation of an incentive. Some of my friends joined me in sneaking into Descanso Gardens through a culvert coming from the cement wash that went through it. We had a great time being there — we thought we had beaten the system! But when we left, we found out that there was no admission charge. The excitement of sneaking in quickly diminished and was replaced with disappointment.

In 2016, I took a vacation and traveled to Egypt. I noticed that many people lived on the first and second floors of four-story houses, where the third and fourth floors were still only outlined in rebar. The reason? Owners are not required to pay property taxes on unfinished houses. So there was an incentive never to finish construction. Similarly, when I traveled to Italy, I noticed that instead of real windows, many houses simply had windows painted on the outside of them. And what was the reason for that? Property taxes were computed by the number of actual windows on a house. So painted windows maintained the outside symmetry of the house, but taxes on the houses were reduced.

All of this means that government, along with everyone else, should be aware of the incentives they are creating. Dr. Friedman taught us that "We get more of what we subsidize and less of what we tax." So, what are we subsidizing today in large part? Victimization, excuses, and lack of productivity. And what are we taxing? Success. And what are we getting more of? That answer is obvious. Dr. Friedman further asserted that "We should judge our programs by their results, not their good intentions." This approach also would counteract the multiple times that, when something goes wrong in society, politicians have almost a universal tendency simply to pass another law to address it. It doesn't particularly matter if the law works, but only that politicians are seen as "doing something." If placed into effect, Dr. Friedman's change in approach would cause a positive revolution in government.

Libertarians believe in accountability at all levels of government. A Libertarian government would provide for regular public audits of all government agencies, as well as "Sunset Provisions" that would require each government agency, individually and publicly on a scheduled basis, to get a vote from Congress to justify its budget and even its existence by demonstrating its past accomplishments, money spent in that process and future goals and the proposed budget therefor. At the very least, this would result in leaner and more cost-effective and transparent governments, and go a long way in reducing government deficits.

When I served as a Peace Corps volunteer in Palmar Norte, Costa Rica, I taught physical education as a *professor de educacion' fi'sica* in its one high school. Additionally, I oversaw programs of community recreation and health, often wearing a white tennis hat and carrying my white-faced monkey named Homer on my shoulder. (So I really blended in.) Though Homer's name did not bestow him with the literary ability and prowess of his namesake, he stood witness to many lessons I learned. One of those lessons is that people will not change their attitudes, actions, or thoughts unless there's a "felt need." How do I benefit from this change? How does my family benefit from this change? As you will discover in the pages of this book, the Libertarian platform offers concrete solutions to problems that are not being addressed. Hopefully, you will walk away with a felt need and a desire to sow the seeds of change with me.

Chapter 2

Libertarian Thought and the Libertarian Party: A Tour D'horizon

So, where did we come from exactly? The Libertarian Party in the United States was formed in Colorado during the winter of 1971 with Mr. David Nolan at the helm. But before diving into the history of the Libertarian Party, which is much younger than Libertarian thought, let's go back to the sixth century B.C., when the Chinese philosopher Lao Tzu made a poignant assertion. He wrote, "Without law or compulsion, men would dwell in harmony." This idea migrated to Western civilizations and, ironically, China as we know it today may very well be the antithesis of Tzu's ancient wisdom: which makes it an Orwellian nightmare.

People typically associate Libertarianism with economic freedom. However, history tells us that the roots of this philosophy encompassed religious tolerance as well. Around A.D. 200, a man named Tertullian was cultivating a theory of toleration as an alternative to the pervasive persecution Christians were enduring by the Roman State. He wrote, "It is a fundamental human right, a privilege of nature, that every man should worship according to his own convictions. One man's religion neither harms nor helps another man. It is assuredly no part of religion to compel religion, to which free will and not force should lead us."

Religious persecution, unfortunately, did not end after Tertullian's time. If it had, the world would obviously be a very different place. I have worked hard to engage religious scholars of many faiths to write articles about the commonalities of the world's religions. Of course, we all know there are differences, and those differences have spawned wars, revolutions, and other violence, and are well-documented in the world's history. What our group is trying to do is to stress the many commonalities that the world religions share. You can find these articles at www.Pro-JectUnderstanding.com. It is our hope that these essays, by shedding more light on the enormous commonalities between religious and spiritual traditions, will help to guide us all to a deeper sense of calm, peace, and understanding.

St. Thomas Aquinas, who lived in the 13th century, was a Catholic theologian whose contributions remain of much significance today. He too posited an argument in favor of limiting royal power when he wrote, "A king who is unfaithful to his duty forfeits his claim to obedience. It is not rebellion to depose him, for he is himself a rebel whom the nation has a right to put down. But it is better to abridge his power, that he may be unable to abuse it."

John Locke wrote in 1690 in *The Second Treatise of Civil Government* that "Every Man has a Property in his own Person. This no Body has any Right to but himself. The Labour of his Body, and the Work of his Hands, we may say, are properly his. Whatsoever then he removes out of the State that Nature hath provided, and left it in, he hath mixed his Labour with, and joyned to it something that is his own, and thereby makes it his Property." Our nation's Founders relied a great deal upon John Locke and his teachings.

Adam Smith's *The Wealth of Nations* was considered a blueprint for the modern discipline of economics, as it well explained what happens when you leave people alone: thriving capitalism. He first coined the term "the Invisible Hand" and conceptualized it as a metaphor for the forces that we cannot see that move the free market economy. With freedom of production and consumption in a society made up of self-interested individuals, the entire system benefits.

As such, Smith developed a theory in economics as a spontaneous order. Thus, instead of governments imposing order, he argued that if we were to allow people to interact with one another freely while protecting their rights to Liberty and property, centrally directed order will necessarily emerge. Take the market economy, for example. Every single day countless people enter marketplaces hoping to make a profit from their labors and skills to build a better life for themselves and their families. By engaging in production and trade, wealth can be built indeed.

Whether you were aware of this or not, Liberty is fundamental to the United States of America. In 1776 the American colonies said adieu to Great Britain with our Declaration of Independence, perhaps the most exceptional example of Libertarian thought ever committed to paper. In that magnificent document, Thomas Jefferson famously wrote, "WE hold these truths to be self-evident, that all Men are created equal, that they are endowed by their Creator with certain unalienable Rights, that among these are Life, Liberty, and the Pursuit of Happiness — That to secure these Rights, Governments are instituted among Men, deriving their just Powers from the Consent of the Governed, that whenever any Form of Government becomes destructive of these Ends, it is the Right of the People to alter or abolish it..."

In sum, Jefferson makes three points. One, people have natural rights. Two, the government's purpose is to protect these rights. Three, if the government overreaches beyond this purpose, people have the right to change it or get rid of it and replace it with something better. The American Revolution, at its ideological core, was a battle for freedom that culminated from a deep distrust of power. Power was seen as a necessary evil that must be limited, controlled, and restricted in every way possible.

After the independent Americans obtained their military victory over Great Britain those ideas that justified the call to arms were expressed in numbers of ways. For example, our written Constitution expressly established the separation of powers, and the Bill of Rights. The Framers of the Constitution did not seek to establish a monarchy, nor did they indulge in an unlimited democracy. Instead, the powers of the federal government were carefully enumerated in Article I, Section 8 of the Constitution. To our Founders, Liberty was something for which they risked their treasure and even their lives. Thomas Jefferson often stated his concern that there is a natural progress of government to gain ground and Liberty to yield it. Benjamin Franklin famously warned, as stated above, that anyone who would trade a little less Liberty for a little more security deserves neither. And Thomas Paine notoriously cried out to "Give Me Liberty or Give Me Death!

As I mentioned earlier, my time in the Peace Corps was one of regular learning and left a profound impact on me that persists to this day. Some of the lessons I learned apply to the endurance of our Constitution, as well as situations in which we are trying to institute programs and responses to address problem areas in our world. First, I will repeat the lesson I mentioned at the end of the previous chapter: a program will only be successful if it addresses what we called a "felt need." That means that if the people we are trying to help do not feel from within that there is an important problem to be remedied, the program or response we try to implement will not be successful. And that assuredly is true when we are trying to protect or even maintain our precious Liberties. Our Constitution did not fall from the sky. The parallel between my lessons learned from Peace Corps training and this remarkable document is that it was the product of a need. This "felt need" resulted in a gathering of caring and educated people, uniting under a banner of compromise and a banner of Liberty.

The second lasting lesson I learned as a Peace Corps volunteer is that programs can only really be successful if they will continue on without your involvement. Over the years, I have seen numbers of well thought-out and temporarily successful programs wither and die after the originator was no longer involved. So if what you are addressing needs a temporary fix, go for it. But if what you want is something more lasting, do not wait too long to identify and then groom a successor, as well as the equivalent of a board of directors to ensure that other good people follow thereafter. If you do that, then your program will not have a good chance of being a lasting success. Though the Constitution might not be aptly described as a "program," the document had to meet similar requirements. The Framers did not want a temporary fix. They wanted something permanent.

Thus the Founders had to draft a document that would work, but they also had to draft a document that the states would ratify. So to be successful, they had to compromise, even on some important things. But the main issue, as aforementioned, was tackling the deep mistrust of power that spurred the American Revolution. This new experiment of Self-Government was carefully embarked upon, putting into place provisions to prevent any one person or group to become too powerful, thereby controlling our government and safeguarding our Liberty.

John Adams' philosophical and practical writing in developing the Massachusetts Constitution was drawn upon to cultivate a governing structure that attempted to balance power. Thus each of the three branches of government was designed to have a meaningful check upon the two others. Unfortunately, in many ways, we have gotten away from that approach. Here are three recommendations that I am sure John Adams would pass along to us today if he were still here. First, we should emphasize to each member of Congress that Compromise not only is not a dirty word, it is in our nation's heritage. Second, we should remind our presidential candidates that they are not running for King or Queen. They are simply running to be the head of the Executive Branch. Third, we should strongly resist all efforts to politicize our Judiciary. As citizens of the greatest country in the history of the world, we have a duty to protect and maintain the liberties and form of government bequeathed to us by John Adams and the other Founders. To put it more directly, we deserve the government we get, and if it isn't working, we have no one to blame but ourselves.

Jean-Jacques Rousseau once said that "I prefer Liberty with danger to peace with slavery." What Rousseau refers to as 'Liberty with danger,' I refer to as the Liberty to Fail. I have two friends whom I met while I was a federal prosecutor in the United States Attorney's Office in Los Angeles. After they left office, they formed a law partnership together, but their real passion was in establishing a restaurant. So they created one and tried to make it work, but it didn't. Undaunted, they continued to practice law to support themselves and their dream and tried again — with the same result. Unfazed, they tried it a third time, and now they are the owners of California Pizza Kitchen. (They don't practice law anymore.)

My friends demonstrated the result of having the Liberty to Fail. They were able to develop the Grit to succeed because no one stepped in to shield them from their prior failures. Unfortunately, today's children are often subjected to "hovering" or "helicopter" parents. Though much of this is a product of good intentions, the result often is that children are deprived of developing their own Grit. Psychologist Angele Duckworth defines that Grit as "perseverance, plus the exclusive pursuit of a single passion." And if children, or anyone else, are deprived of the opportunity of experiencing setbacks, much less overcoming them, the odds of developing that Grit — that "spit in your eye" attitude — will be seriously diminished. Struggling is often not a signal for alarm, because tackling problems that exceed one's current skillset can be a good thing. As outlined in the previous chapter, I do hold that society should implement a Safety Net below which no one should be allowed to fall. But that should not be utilized to deprive our people — young and old — of the Liberty to Fail.

In the 19th century, there was rapid technological development. Americans welcomed the railroad and the steam engine, electricity and the internal combustion engine, the telegraph, and the telephone. Alongside these drastic changes to life, Libertarian thought continued to blossom. Much was whispered about a free American society, and in 1834 Alexis de Tocqueville traveled from France to see it in action. Between 1834 and 1840, he observed and worked on his book that was widely successful, *Democracy in America*. In it he praised the experiment of democracy, but cautioned that it would probably work until American politicians discovered that they could buy the citizens votes with their own tax money. That caution should be even more strongly emphasized in our politics today!

Jeremy Bentham proposed a theory of utilitarianism that the government should base its decision-making upon what results in "the greatest happiness for the greatest number." Though he stood on a different footing on natural rights, his ideas of free markets and limited government were a continuation of Libertarian thought. And then there was also the influential John Stuart Mill, who made a compelling argument in 1859 in favor of individual freedom in his highly-regarded book *On Liberty*.

At this point in history, Frederic Bastiat was curating and publishing his work. A member of the French parliament and an economist, Bastiat observed the slippery slope of socialism play out in front of him. What he witnessed was what he described as "legal plunder." What this means is the manipulation of the law, institutions, and systems by one group to redistribute wealth, property, and power to another group. He asserted that, "The state is the great fictitious entity by which everyone seeks to live at the expense of everyone else." Bastiat further argued that laws should never force or compel people to behave in a certain way. The only function of laws should be to prevent harmful actions toward individuals and their property. Toward that end, he wrote:

"When law and force keep a person within the bounds of justice, they impose nothing but a mere negation. They oblige him only to abstain from harming others. They violate neither his personality, his Liberty, nor his property. They safeguard all these... But when the law, by means of its necessary agent, force, imposes upon men a regulation of labor, a method or a subject of education, a religious faith or creed — then the law is no longer negative; it acts positively upon people."

Jim Turney, the Libertarian Party Commissioner of Altamonte Springs, Florida and a friend of mine, attributes his eventual membership and involvement in the Libertarian Party to Bastiat's *The Law*, which was published as a pamphlet in 1850. He was tasked with reading a book in French and writing a report about it. Clever as ever, Jim saw a book that was "translated from French," which happened to be Bastiat's publication. He unassumingly bought it from a bookstore in an attempt to outsmart his French teacher.

But my friend Jim got a bit more than the "Easy A" he bargained for because The Law surprised and captivated him. Bastiat advocated for a just system of laws that, if implemented, would support a free society. Bastiat captured Jim with his lucidity and brutal honesty, often pointing to the shared humanity we have, and pointing out that if the natural tendencies of mankind are so bad that it is not safe to permit people to be free, how is it that the tendencies of these governmental organizers are always so good? Do not the legislators and their appointed agents also belong to the human race? Or do they believe that they themselves are made of "a finer clay" than the rest of mankind?

Perhaps the people in government do believe that they are somehow made of finer clay. Since the time of FDR, the presidency has usurped to itself or has been abrogated by Congress increasingly large amounts of power. In fact, in many ways it has been turned into an Imperial Presidency. But we should all be reminded that we do not have a monarchy in this country. Instead, we have a democracy based upon the Separation of Powers as expressly set forth in our Constitution. This works for the benefit and protection of us all. Thus, as an important example, a president should not be able to send our military troops into combat in places like Korea, Vietnam, Serbia, Panama, Somalia, Iraq, or Afghanistan for more than 60 days without a formal Declaration of War being passed by Congress.

My friend and former Republican Congressman Tom Campbell, who graced us all with his Preface to this book, took issue with this as well. In 1999, he challenged President Bill Clinton's war in the former Yugoslavia, which he argued was unconstitutionally conducted. There was no Declaration of War or other Congressional authorization, but the courts made one thing abundantly clear: they upheld Clinton's powers to wage war. Thus, as a practical matter today, presidents can initiate and conduct wars whenever they please. In this respect, we have allowed the Founder's intention of a system of checks and balances to fail. It's a collapse of constitutional principles, and more people need to pay attention to it.

This entitlement of those in power has encroached upon other liberties as well, namely when it comes to our election donation laws. I start with the premise that wealthy people who want to donate money to their favorite candidates or issues will, as a practical matter, always be able to do so. Maybe not directly, but through PACs, which are (supposedly) independent expenditures, or various other means. In addition, if wealthy people are candidates themselves, they are allowed to make unlimited contributions to their own campaigns.

What has been the result? Much chicanery by wealthy people, unfair advantages for the wealthy as candidates, and it has required most candidates who are not wealthy themselves to spend much of their time trying to raise small donations from lots of other people.

And how does one raise money? Often by direct mailers that attempt to appeal to the recipients on one particular emotional issue that simultaneously vilifies their opponents on that same issue. Those approaches to fundraising have strongly contributed to the polarization that is now prevalent in our country.

So what should be done? If Bill Gates could spend as much money as he would want on his own election campaign, he should also be able to spend all he wants for other candidates or issues of his choice as well. It's all a matter of free speech and Liberty! However, all contributions above a certain fairly small threshold amount should immediately be disclosed both to the government election commissions and publicly on the internet. Then, for example, if voters believe that a recipient candidate is "in Bill Gates' pocket," they can always vote for that candidate's opponent. However, no non-human entities should be allowed to contribute to any candidates or initiatives whatsoever. Why is that? It's also a matter of Liberty. If corporations contribute money, they should first get the unanimous consent of their shareholders because they are spending their shareholders' money. And often, those shareholders do not support that particular candidate or cause. Of course, corporations would always be free to appeal to their shareholders to contribute their own personal money if they wanted, but that would be all they should be able to do. The same thing goes for labor unions or any other entities. This approach, engaging Liberty, would reduce the chicanery, unfairness, polarization, and frustration that are heavily present in our elections at this time, and it would also increase freedom of choice. So, once again, Liberty works!

Considering this deep entrenchment of Libertarian thought in America's DNA, it's time for the Libertarian Party to be recognized as the most intrinsically American political party. Without consistent efforts to preserve or restore Liberty where it has been lost, the way forward will be a path our Founders would wish we hadn't taken.

As you've been able to glean so far, Libertarian principles have a rich history. So, what about the Libertarian Party's history here in the United States? As mentioned at the beginning of this chapter, the Libertarian Party was founded in December of 1971. But a series of meetings were held earlier that summer in Westminster, Colorado, gatherings which were fueled by a disdain for Nixon's policies, such as our involvement in the Vietnam "conflict," and a refusal to sit back and accept the "new normal" for America.

In the midst of Vietnam, the dissipating of fiscal conservatism within the Republican Party, and a Democratic Party that was growing increasingly socialist, the group considered creating an alternative choice. They felt a growing sense of urgency that peaked after Nixon's speech in 1971, where he announced the implementation of wage and price controls, thereby effectively replacing the gold standard.

But why does that matter? The answer is that wage and price controls make it far easier for the government to condone inflation. Nolan and others formed the LP as an official party just a few months later, an attempt to initiate America's departure from the left/right paradigm we still remain attached to today. In 1969, two years before the formation of the LP, Nolan had developed a Cartesian Coordinate Chart, which is a simple way to measure political affiliation. There's also a quiz that goes along with it, which measures one's opinions on economic and personal freedoms and determines a political affiliation reflective of the quiz-taker's answers. Two years later, Nolan's simple diagram was finally in the process of materializing on the political stage.

The LP held its first convention in 1972 in the City of Denver. It was a small inaugural event, attended by about 85 people. They started planning vigorously, organizing themselves into a loose network of state parties, with an elected central committee overseeing the network. They also established organizational bylaws and cultivated a platform standing mainly in three important issues. First, calling for the withdrawal of all United States troops from Vietnam. Second, the abolition of victimless crimes and the Federal Communications Commission, and third: draft amnesty. After the convention, the new Libertarian Party released a formal statement: "We, the members of the Libertarian Party, challenge the cult of the omnipotent state and defend the rights of the individual."

The party had officially stepped into electoral politics, and the rate of growth in the first few years was extraordinary. By the time of the Denver convention in June 1972, the party had 1000 members. A few months later, on election day, that number doubled. A year later, party membership was around 3000 members, and there were Libertarian organizations in thirty-two states. That election of 1972 had a Libertarian ticket on the ballot in two states: Colorado and Washington. John Hospers, a philosophy professor at the University of Southern California, ran for president, and Toni Nathan, a businesswoman and broadcast journalist in Oregon, was his running mate. They had a campaign budget of less than $7000, but they earned 2,671 votes, and one electoral vote, which spurred a wave of media coverage.

The electoral vote was cast by Roger MacBride, a former Republican, who abandoned his party's ticket in favor of the

Hospers/Nathan ticket. That was an important moment for many reasons. Among those was that it propelled the Libertarian Party into the national news cycle, and it resulted in Toni Nathan being the first woman to receive an electoral college vote. The ideological zeal of the 1960s and 1970s was used as an opportunity to offer the American People an alternative to the chaos we'd reluctantly become accustomed to.

MacBride's contribution to the growth of the Libertarian Party led to his eventual campaign for president himself in 1976 as a Libertarian. He embraced the opportunity, spending $500,000 on his own campaign (which pales in comparison to Bloomberg's short-lived $500 million self-funded campaign in 2020, although MacBride's investment raised eyebrows back in those days). He had his own converted DC-3 plane, which he piloted through forty-eight states. The party also used television advertisements as well, fully leveraging the FCC rules for equal airtime. The results reflected these efforts, as MacBride earned 173,000 votes and was on thirty-two state ballots. Seeing this growth, the appetite for political victory grew stronger.

Soon brothers David and Charles Koch began funding Libertarian causes, which also gave birth to The Cato Institute, a think tank that supplies education and ideas to policymakers. The Libertarian Party and The Cato Institute started approaching the reach of Libertarian ideas in tandem, though from different vantage points. Where the LP was concerned with political traction, Cato modeled as a practical example for the serious and engaged Libertarians.

Much progress was made during the 1960s and 70s, though that dropped off when the party fell victim to a disappointing election outcome in 1980, when Ed Clark's Libertarian bid for the presidency was met with a total of 921,000 votes, just short of the million they hoped for. 1980 was also the year that The Statue of Liberty was adopted as the official party symbol. At this point, supporters and party insiders started to drift off, and the party fell victim to infighting, which chipped away and slowly deteriorated the organizational vehicle that was crucial to effective advocacy for political change. But the groundswell resumed because, by 1985, 49 Libertarians around the country were in elective office.

1987 marked a further rebound for Libertarian efforts. It was the year Dr. Ron Paul left the Republican Party and joined the Libertarian Party. It was also the year that Libertarians in Big Water, Utah won every city council seat. In 1990, Libertarian Nancy Lord Taker ran for mayor in Washington, DC. Six years later, the LP celebrated its 25th anniversary, and in 1998, the African-American civil rights leader Roy Innis gave the LP further credibility by joining forces with it.

As stated above, I joined the Libertarian Party in 2001 following the passage of the so-called Patriot Act. I proudly ran for Vice President in 2012, alongside former New Mexico Governor Gary Johnson. We both traveled all over the country but, although we received good local news coverage wherever we went, we almost never received any national coverage. I am also proud to say that wherever I went, I was picked up by people, who I called my mother hens, and driven at their own expense and often for days to our events. These were some of the finest, most aware, and caring people I have ever met, and I would place them up against any other people in political life. But there simply were not enough of them. We received more than 1.2 million votes in that election, which was double what our candidates had received in 2008. But, since I considered us to be the most qualified candidates in the election, I was disappointed — and I remain so.

But as our country continues down a path of deep polarization and personality politics, the growing public disillusionment with government as it now is might generate some new interest in viable third party candidates. And that is what happened in the 2016 election, in which Governors Gary Johnson and Bill Weld received a total of just under 4.5 million votes, which was 3.27 percent of the total vote nationwide.

Chapter 3

Liberty and Justice

What's the most important thing in life? My answer is gratification. It's not power, it's not prestige, it's not money, it's not even love. It's because the world has been made into a somewhat better place because you have been here. To me that is the best feeling in the world, and it's one of few reasons why I pursued a career in the Justice System.

Another reason was my father, Judge William P. Gray, who was a highly regarded federal district court judge, and he remains one of my biggest heroes. As an example, a long time ago when he was a judge and I was a prosecutor in the Los Angeles Federal Courthouse, I would continually see him not only greeting the custodians in the hallways, but even asking about their children — all by name! And the custodians would literally glow in response. It was not his way to speak to me about things like this, instead he led by example. So I started doing the same thing. Amazingly enough, the first time I did this was to the custodian who was cleaning my office in the same courthouse. When I greeted him by name, which I knew from the label on his shirt, he literally stopped in his tracks. Then the man told me that he had been working here for ten years and that I was the first attorney ever to address him by name. The irony of this was that I eventually learned that he was the father of one of the stars on the

UCLA Basketball team. So that was my unneeded tangible reward for treating people as people.

The fundamental truth is that people everywhere simply want to be treated with dignity, and most people will respond accordingly when that happens. So this brings me to another story about my father. One weekend he went up to Lompoc Federal Prison to take a tour, and he happened to take my wonderful mother along with him. As my mother later recounted, during the tour the warden said that there would be a talent show that afternoon presented by some of the inmates and asked if they would like to attend. Sure, was the answer. So before the show began, my father was sitting in the first row, with the warden on one side of him and my mother on the other. And next to my mother was an inmate, who struck up a conversation by saying: "Mrs. Gray, I'm sure you don't know this, but your husband was the judge who sentenced me to be here," whereupon my mother became a bit uncomfortable. The inmate continued: "Yes, and he actually gave me a maximum sentence," whereupon my mother started leaning over toward my father. "But," the inmate went on, "Judge Gray treated me with such respect during all of the proceedings, that he is my favorite judge — and I have had lots of judges!" Bottom line: treating people as people works, for everyone. So please join me in saying hello to the people who clean our hotel rooms and mow our grass, as well as those who are in wheelchairs or are in other ways disabled. They are anxious simply to be recognized as the human beings they are, and we are blessed to have the Liberty to do just that!

Beginning in September of 1968, after my Peace Corps service ended, I attended the USC School of Law. This really was quite a change because I was thrown into a highly competitive and stressful situation within seven days of my return from Costa Rica. In addition, since I received my 1A military draft classification as well as a notice to take a physical examination within two weeks of returning home, I knew what my future had in store for me since this was in the height of the Vietnam War. So I had three choices about my future. First, I could be drafted as an enlisted man and "swab the decks" for two years and then come back after my service for my last two years of law school. Second, I could go into the Naval Reserve Officers Training Corps (NROTC) at USC, finish law school and then become a line officer and "sail the seas" for three years. Or, third, I could "double down" and apply for and join the Judge Advocate General's Corps (JAG) and be a Navy attorney for four years. I decided upon the latter choice and actually get some professional benefit from my service, and I have always been glad about that choice. But, among other things, that meant that I would be marching in drill formation with an M-1 rifle over my shoulder with lots of freshmen every Thursday for my last two years of law school, as well as studying lots of "useful" things like celestial navigation so I could locate where the ship was at night if the stars were visible.

Some people through my lifetime have labeled me as an "outside agitator in disguise," and I think at times I have given them some ammunition, because in May 1970, toward the end of my second year of law school, I led a peace march from the campus of USC to the steps of the Los Angeles City Hall. Once there, we first protested and then sent about 20,000 signed letters to President Nixon demanding that he remove our troops from Cambodia. Then, in one of the true ironies of my life, I was sent on a summer midshipman "training cruise" on the U.S.S. Meeker County, which was a Landing Ship Tank (LST 980), from Guam to the rivers of Vietnam. So I went from a peace march to a combat zone, while barely having a chance, for you who know the game of Monopoly, to "Pass Go." As far as I know, I am only one of two people in the history of the United States Navy to be awarded Vietnam Service and Combat Action Ribbons on a training cruise.

Fresh out of law school, and after passing the California bar exam, I was stationed on independent duty at the U.S. Naval Air Station in Guam. The most meaningful part of my service was when I took a transport plane to an orphanage in Danang, Vietnam, where my first wife and I adopted my son Ky. The reason we pursued an adoption was that we both agreed that zero population growth was a good thing, and she had been adopted herself. So we wrote to every Vietnamese orphanage we could find, with absolutely no response. Then one day a woman came to me for legal assistance in providing her the legal pleadings necessary for the adoption of her son, who was to arrive from Vietnam the next week. Of course, I agreed and did so. But I also told her our desires to adopt and asked how she had been successful. She responded that she wrote to the orphanages. But when I said we had too she responded, "Oh no, you write in French." Why? Because French was the second language of most of the Catholic nuns, and English was a distant third. So she wrote a letter in French for us, we signed it, and the Sacred Heart Orphanage soon set aside our potential son for us.

Ky arrived on a Pan Am flight on August 10, 1973, at the approximate age of 13 months. (When I visited the orphanage, I tried to discover any information I could about his background, but no one knew anything, including his original name, age, birthdate or parents.) But physically he was a wreck, in that even at 13 months he couldn't crawl or even hold his head up more than half of time, and he also had several ear infections and was acutely malnourished, with the accompanying bloated stomach and thin extremities.

As a stroke of sheer coincidence, my parents were visiting us on Guam when Ky arrived, so they were present with us at the airport to pick him up. (There was only one federal judge on Guam, and my father sat for him while he took his yearly vacation.) But then, with love, the stimulation of his parents and his brother who was three months younger, as well as solid medical attention, Ky took his first steps on Christmas Eve, just four and a half months later. That was truly an amazing and welcome transformation!

So we were truly pleased with Ky's physical transformation, but what was even more pleasing was what we saw about his mental adjustments. They were exemplified one day while we were still in Guam when Ky was entertaining himself by rocking on a ball that had bells inside of it. Of course, we were concerned when we saw our son Billy come up to him and take the ball away without any response at all from Ky. But soon we saw that Ky had crawled into the kitchen, fetched Billy's "sacred" blue blanket and came back with it into the den. When Billy saw Ky with his blanket he gasped, dropped the ball and went for his blanket. So Ky simply went back to rocking on his ball. With that we knew that Ky would be just fine!

Ky was never interested in Vietnam or the Vietnamese or their customs or culture. We never pushed that upon him, but I told him that if he ever wanted to go back, I would take him. So finally, in March 2016, after telling me he wanted to see where he came from, I took him back to North Vietnam and his orphanage in Danang. We actually found Sister Teresa, one of the nuns who had cared for him, was still there. Tears flowed! Then we walked across the street to China Beach where I had carried Ky when I first had visited the orphanage and, putting my hurting back at risk, I reached down and again picked up my son. So now I have a picture of me carrying Ky at age 4 months and also at 43 years at the same place. And the two nuns with us were laughing big time.

Once I returned to civilian life, and as I said above, I served as an Assistant U.S. Attorney in Los Angeles, eventually heading a unit that prosecuted frauds on the Veterans Administration and Federal Housing Administration. I then worked in a civil law firm for about six years before Governor Deukmejian appointed me as a judge of the Orange County Municipal Court in Santa Ana, California. Then, after six years, I was elevated to the Superior Court, where I served for an additional nineteen years. During that time, I sat on every calendar in the Superior Court except family law.

When I retired from the Orange County Superior Court, I was recruited by Ms. Lucie Barron, the owner of ADR Services, Inc., which stands for Alternative Dispute Resolution. To this day, I work as a private judge for mediations, arbitrations, and as a discovery referee. Lucie, whom I greet with "Hi Boss," is not a lawyer by training, she is a psychologist. But she started ADR Services because she had gotten involved in a legal dispute and she thought it could have been handled better and more efficiently. She didn't know much about the law, but did know how to be an effective entrepreneur. So she started up a competing business, all from scratch. She started by going to the UCLA business school and started reading California's Code of Civil Procedure, which gave her the legal vernacular she was looking for. "We are the peace makers," is what she says.

The field of private mediation has now become an adjunct to the courts, which in many ways could not survive without the resources provided by the private sector, and Lucie's company has grown to be the second largest in the industry in California. What we do there is both to help people to receive justice and also to feel like they have received justice. And Lucie's endeavor also demonstrates some of our Libertarian principles in action: competition in the free market is essential to a prosperous society. Where the courts are unable to be efficient and effective due to a lack of resources, the private sector provides viable alternatives (at least to those who can afford our services).

I am deeply proud to be and to have been a part of the System of Justice in the United States of America. I believe that the more people see and understand what we do, the more they will be proud of us as well. Fundamentally, the Justice System is an institution that protects all of us from harm and resolves disputes at every level in society. But our system is constantly evolving. In most matters, I believe we are going in the right direction, but in some matters, I believe we are not.

As a reality, the practical definition of Justice is whatever the king or ruler says it is. But in our country, it comes from "We the People." In addition, in many ways, Justice means Foreseeability, which is to say that if you do this, then that is the likely result. So, you can plan accordingly and thereby mostly stay out of trouble. The injustices, then, are seen as when you do what you were told was lawful, and then the rules are changed or not followed, and you are punished. In my view, the purpose of the criminal justice system is to reduce crime and all of the harm and misery that accompany it. There must be negative consequences for criminal acts but, as a practical matter, it is not possible to accomplish these worthwhile goals through punishment alone.

This view is held by most Libertarians, who believe that our justice system too often imposes too many punishments that outweigh the crimes committed. As stated above, Adam Smith thought of justice as a concept that is strictly negative in nature, something that must be attained by abstaining from violations of our Liberties, such as theft or coercion. In *The Theory of Moral Sentiments* he wrote: "The rules that call loudest for vengeance and punishment are the laws which guard the life and person of our neighbor; the next are those which guard his property and possessions; and last of all come those which guard what are called his personal rights, or what is due to him from the promises of others." We need justice to hold a line of societal effectiveness and stability. In this Libertarian view, the state acts as an arbitrator, which should be an impartial entity that allows for cooperation and productivity between and among citizens, like a referee in an athletic competition.

I wrote a musical about our 1787 Constitutional Convention. Among the things I learned from researching and then writing Convention: The Birth of America, is that, of course, the delegates debated, argued and even fought about many issues at that convention: the rights of big states versus small; to have a standing army or not; whether the federal government should have control over the states and, if so, how much and in what areas; and, of course, slave states or free? But the ONE thing that ALL delegates agreed upon was that THE most important function of government was to protect our freedoms and liberties against the encroachment of government. (The second-most important thing was keeping us safe.) So how far have we strayed from our Founders' primary objective of our government? Suffice it to say that I deeply believe that our Founders would be deeply disappointed in us.

But there are some groups that are doing our Founders proud in fighting for and upholding our Liberties. As stated above, one is the CATO Institute, but another is the Institute for Justice. Since 1991, IJ has successfully taken on cases at no charge to the litigants to keep the government from unduly condemning people's lands without even having a purpose in mind for its later use; forfeiting a man's $42,000 truck based upon a conviction involving possessing about $200 worth of illicit drugs; requiring people to have a government license before they can work as tour guides; enforcing a term of probation that prohibited a defendant from writing a book about how the Securities Exchange Commission over-prosecuted his own case; and upholding parents' ability to choose where government money is to be spent for the education of their children, even if it happens to be at a military, religious or vocational school. These groups deserve our praise and our support. So, if you wish to join me in thanking and supporting IJ, please visit its website at www.IJ.org.

Calls for justice are frequent in our current media cycle. After the tragic murder of George Floyd, scores of protestors took to the streets across our nation, often chanting "No Justice, No Peace." So let us learn from George Floyd and, tragically, from many others like him who have been wrongly harmed by the police. These recent events remind me of a book that was given to me last year entitled *Just Mercy: A Story of Justice and Redemption* by Bryan Stevenson. The person who gave it to me said she had read it and thought of me.

I was flattered, because this is a book about an attorney/author in the Alabama and Georgia areas who filed appeals on death penalty cases and told us about the stories and players surrounding them. Mr. Stevenson asserts there have been many atrocious cases in those states even into the late 1980s in which African-Americans were put to death for crimes for which they were factually innocent. The existence of just one of those cases is simply too much, but there were many. And even if their guilt was fairly established, the book quoted the statistic that a Black man was eleven times more likely in those states to receive a death penalty sentence if his victim had been a Caucasian instead of the victim being Black. This fact cannot make us proud!

Many people in the African-American community are terrified of the police and the court system — and often for good reasons. How can we respond? By seeking justice. Let's insist that all police officers wear body cameras whenever they interact with the public. That will result in both the officers and the people they serve being more accountable and even respectful. Let's also reduce the ability of police unions (a public service union feared by many, including FDR) to keep misbehaving officers from being punished or fired. Let's insist that police be trained to be more aware of methods to scale down confrontations so that violence is much less likely. This should include training about how to have more racial and foreign heritage awareness, and also how to detect and deal with people with mental disabilities or drug addictions. Or, better yet, develop other types of agencies to deal on the streets with the mentally ill, drug-addicted and homeless, which will leave the police more opportunity to investigate and prosecute things like robbery, rape, murder, theft, and fraud.

The courts play a role here too. If one looks back into history and thinks about it, had racial integration been left up to the will of an opinion poll instead of an independent judiciary, we probably would probably have been operating with an officially segregated society for a lot longer period of time than we did. Thus the courts should be viewed as a bastion that protects our cherished freedoms from the excesses of the majority. (That is why we call our system of government a republic instead of a democracy. As Benjamin Franklin once described it, "Democracy is two wolves and a lamb voting upon what to have for dinner. A republic gives the well-armed the means to contest the vote.")

Do you want more Equal Justice for All?, then let's repeal our failed policy of Drug Prohibition, which has militarized the police and caused them to be seen by many residents in minority communities as being an occupational force (See Chapter 11, infra.). And let's all do our part by trying to be more sensitive to each other's views and needs. But, at the same time, let's also understand that police have truly difficult jobs, and sometimes they must face difficult and even dangerous situations that can call for instantaneous decisions to be made at their peril. So, let's take that into account when sitting in judgment about their actions.

In other words, let us all intentionally choose not to go down the road of "We are Good, and You are Evil." We are in this together — as Americans! We must acknowledge our failings, but also continue to strive to be United in Liberty — and in the Responsibility that goes with it. Polarization may sometimes make good politics but, in the end, it harms us all. Instead let's all strive to invoke the spirit of Dr. Martin Luther King, who said: "Yes, if you want to say that I was a drum major, say that I was a drum major for justice, drum major for peace (and) drum major for righteousness." That is what America stands for, and that's what we now must do, be drum majors for the great things our country represents — together! That is actually the American Way!

Nevertheless, there also comes a time when all Americans of Good Will must take a stand about the dissension now existing in our country. And the first thing that must be said here is that, unless my eyes were deceiving me, the murder of George Floyd at the hands of the Minneapolis policemen was a horrendous and unforgiveable criminal act. But it is hard to conclude that the act was caused by systematic racism by that city's police — particularly since the chief of police at the time was African-American. And it is similarly hard to conclude that there is systematic racism in many other cities like Chicago, Detroit, New York, and Cleveland that are completely governed by people who profess to be liberals. Nevertheless, we do have a history of programmed racism in our country, such as the abominable way we treated Native Americans, slavery before the Civil War, and Jim Crow's harsh injustices, and even lynchings thereafter, mistreatment of Chinese workers building the railroads and, of course, the internment camps for the Japanese-Americans during World War II. These must be openly acknowledged and even fully discussed and taught.

But, having said that, much of this friction appears to have developed into a political climate of "Us vs. Them," which is cancerous. Yes, Equal Justice for All is a bedrock principle that must govern our country, but being "politically correct" has in many too many ways become pervasive. For example, the brilliant economist Thomas Sowell, who happens to be African-American, recently expressed his astonishment that some people were being forced to apologize for things that happened before they were born, but others were not being held accountable for their own looting and arson. Similarly, the star professional football quarterback Drew Brees was forced, seemingly at the peril of losing his career, to recant his standing up for the flag of our country when he said that it reminded him of the sacrifices of people like his grandfather during World War II.

Yes, some bad things have happened in this country that was established and has been run by people with defects. But the flag of the United States of America stands for our founding principle of Liberty — and our Constitution actually holds for the proposition that people have the freedom to burn or otherwise desecrate that flag if that is their choice — talk about Liberty. In other words, we are still "Becoming America." America itself is a perfect idea, but the United States of America is still, and probably always be, a Work in Progress.

Inside of the court system, many experienced judges understand that we must employ the concept of "Restorative Justice." And these judges also understand the importance of rehabilitation, treatment, and community healing in that effort. The fundamental basis for this approach is to bring the victim(s) of an offense and the perpetrator(s) together, face to face, in a meeting monitored by a therapist. The emphasis is basically to show the offenders what effects the incident had upon the victims, on the one hand, and to explore the concept of understanding and even forgiveness by the victims, on the other. Thus, the intent is both to humanize the act in the eyes of the offender(s) and to begin an important healing process for the victim(s). We are seeing success a great amount of the time in both of those areas, but there still is much room for improvement.

Fundamentally, the purpose of the criminal justice system is not to punish the offender but is instead to reduce crime. A big example of this is in the area of domestic violence. If the batterer (mostly but not always a man) is forced to focus upon the position of the victim, as well as the physical and emotional trauma he has inflicted, statistics show that he is not nearly as likely to re-offend. It is also often quite helpful for the batterers to look back at their own past, because they were often raised in a culture where this type of conduct occurred. In addition, the healing and self-esteem process often get a jumpstart with the education of the victims that they were not the cause of their own harm, which enables them more fully and safely to get on with their lives.

Another critically important part of Restorative Justice is for the victims to be consulted by the court at time of the sentencing of the offender and, if leniency is being considered, this almost always requires the victims' consent. Happily, the approach has also been found to work well with burglaries and even assaults and batteries (although it doesn't seem to work very well with tax offenses). The lesson? Like in many other aspects of life, humanizing the interactions among different parties can go a long way toward reducing friction and harm, and increasing empathy and even harmony. So progress is being made in the criminal justice system, and I thought you should know.

We've all heard much rhetoric from those on the political stage about being "Tough on Crime." However, being tough is not conducive to being just. So I propose an alternative: being "Smart on Crime." There are seven pillars to my vision, the first one being that we need to stop "Over-Criminalization." Many jurisdictions have turned their police and traffic laws into fundraising mechanisms. Not only does this frequently weigh disproportionally upon the poor, it also directly results in anger and distrust against law enforcement in general. In addition, large fines, coupled with additional penalty assessments, often result in unpayable amounts of money being owed by many people. And if the fines are not paid, that inevitably results in additional fines and even being subject to arrest. So, the cycle perpetuates itself.

Second, arrests should be seen as a last resort, just like in medicine where surgery is seen as the last resort. Furthermore, if people are arrested, bail should be reasonable. That includes the proposition that suspects who are not a threat to anyone and are reasonably likely to appear in court should be released upon their written promise to appear. Being jailed pending trial is a major hardship that not only precludes defendants from helping to prepare their own defense, it also all too frequently results in defendants either losing their jobs or unfairly pleading guilty to offenses just so they can get out of jail with "credit for time served."

Third, mandatory minimum sentences should be repealed. No one can determine a reasonable punishment in advance without knowing who the perpetrators are, their backgrounds, who the victims are and how badly, if at all, they were harmed. But these "automatic" punishments often result in obscenely long sentences that are truly unfair to the defendants, their families, and also the taxpayers. And, in addition, just the threat of serving those long sentences is often enough wrongly to coerce defendants into pleading guilty to a lesser offense. This is not justice!

Fourth, and as stated above, body cameras on the uniforms of the police almost always result in better conduct both by the police and also by the people in the community, which is an especially relevant reform in our current times.

The fifth pillar of reform ties right into the fourth, which is community policing. Get the police back to being peace officers instead of law enforcement officers. That includes, again I say, the repeal of the failed policy of the so-called War on Drugs, because that often results in the police treating drug violators like the "enemy."

Sixth, repeal what is sometimes called "Policing for Profit." In other words, change the civil asset forfeiture laws to require a criminal conviction before anyone's property can be forfeited to the government, with the forfeiture issue being presented to the same jury. And when this does occur, the forfeited property must be placed into the general fund instead of police coffers. Clearly, our police must be fully funded for the protection of us all, but they should not have a financial incentive to forfeit people's property.

And, seventh, if nonviolent offenders have drug addictions or mental illness problems, but otherwise are not hurting anyone but themselves, they should be referred to medical professionals, and not to the criminal justice system.

In sum, being "Smart on Crime" instead of "Tough on Crime" means providing reasonable assistance to help people live more productive lives, as well as bringing our police back into the peace officer business. This approach will not only enhance Liberty for everyone, it will make all of us safer, and with the added benefit of reducing taxes along the way.

Chapter 4

Liberty and Incarceration

Fyodor Dostoevsky once said "The degree of civilization in a society can be judged by entering its prisons. A society should be judged not by how it treats its outstanding citizens, but by how it treats its criminals." As members of a civilized society, we have an obligation to treat our prisoners humanely and to keep them safe while they are in our custody, no matter if they are Al Capone or Charles Manson. As long as we meet this threshold of providing them with secure and humane treatment, society deserves to be protected from people who commit criminal violence, and these convicted offenders deserve their fate.

Pat Nolan, a former archconservative member of the California Legislature, had always voted for longer and longer prison sentences for more and more offenders. Actually, that is how he felt until he was himself convicted of an election fraud offense and sentenced to two years in prison. When he emerged from prison, he said that, based upon his direct observations, we have too many people in prison who should not be there. Then he went on to say, "We should reserve our prison space for people we are afraid of, and not people we are mad at." I agree!

Unfortunately, for various reasons, people in our country have seized upon the idea that prisons are the answer to our criminal justice problems. As a result, the United States now leads the world in the incarceration of its people — both in sheer numbers, as well as per capita. But not only is prison the most expensive approach for taxpayers, we must also understand that about 95 percent of the prisoners eventually will be released. So ask yourself the following questions: how well are we doing according to Dostoevsky's standard of measurement? What's going on inside of our prisons? Are we preparing our inmates for life outside of prison once they've served their time?

Although when I was still an active trial court judge in California I had the opportunity of visiting both Norco and San Quentin State Prisons, those threshold tours hardly showed me what prison life was really like. So after I was on the radio show "Coast to Coast with George Noory," talking about the criminal justice system, I thereafter received letters from eleven inmates currently serving time in prisons all around the country. So I took the opportunity to request each of them voluntarily to provide me with their thoughts and experiences of prison life — both the good and the bad. Eight of them agreed, and that is what they did. Take it for what you will, but I strongly believe it is incumbent upon each one of us as citizens to do what we can to ensure that everyone in our custody is treated within reasonably humane degrees of safety, nutrition and welfare. In other words, we all have an obligation to do what we can to make the prison system work. So here is a compilation of the reports from those eight inmates, as well as my recommendations for making some changes.*

----

* What follows was first published in the July, 2021 edition of Verdict Magazine.

Of course, life is different in prison depending upon many things, but the biggest difference comes from the level of security of the prison. Those in low-level security prisons mostly live in military-style barracks, with two-man rooms with bunkbeds and without doors. The days start early, with inmates getting up usually around 5:30 a.m., with breakfast being from 6 to 7. Then jobs, education, physical exercise, and other activities go from about 7 a.m. to 3 p.m. There are frequent body counts during the day in which the inmates must remain standing, and the rest of the day they use "move times" to change locations on the prison "campus." Then dinner is from 6 to 7, with extra time often being given to the cell block that has been judged to be the cleanest for the past week. After dinner, most prisons go into lock-down.

As a further representative example of daily prison life, one inmate reported as follows: The majority of my time is spent to work out each day to maintain my health and mental wellbeing. I do my yoga and practice my Buddhist faith, and try to get as much law library time as possible so that someday I might win 1983s for the benefit of all. (Section 1983 of Title 42 in the United States Code is known as the Civil Rights Act of 1871, which was enacted to combat post-Civil War racial violence in the Southern states and is a primary means of correcting Constitutional violations by state officials.) Everyone complains about the quality of the food, saying it is often stale and even moldy, and mostly a heavy concentration of unhealthy carbohydrates instead of fruits, vegetables, and protein in order to reduce expenses. Sack lunches are usually given out after breakfast and often consist of a bologna sandwich (one slice) and things like pretzels. Dinner often consists of a pressed chicken patty or gravy over white rice with Kool-Aid and Jell-O on the side.

Generally, holidays are not something really celebrated at most prisons, with the exception of a slice of pressed turkey at Thanksgiving, the addition of a slice of ham at Christmas, and two hot dogs on the 4th of July. In addition, frequently the inmates are kept at lockdown during significant holidays because the prisons are usually short-staffed due to their workers trying to take their vacations during those times. But, as one inmate candidly stated, "Can we blame them?"

Most inmates do have access to movies and small televisions, many of which require an FM radio to hear the sound. If internet is available for songs and entertainment, it is "Pay as you go." And weights are also frequently available which, in a men's facility, is often deeply appreciated and they are heavily used. Several inmates stated that often the best time of the week is chapel services, with chaplains addressing all denominations — and often they have libraries!

Many said that in the lower security facilities the walls were cracking, some buildings were condemned and simply abandoned. Other places reeked of raw sewage. To strengthen those points, many inmates said that the prison staff would routinely bring in their own water bottles because of the poor quality of the drinking water. In addition, many expressed the desire to have functioning microwave ovens at their facility to heat their food. As one man said, 190-degree water can be used to cook noodles, but it doesn't work for anything else. And functioning air conditioning was also a common complaint, particularly since many prison facilities are located in desert or semi-desert areas. Some inmates would purchase small fans to help with the heat, but at a cost of $10.95 for a fan and $2.55 for a set of batteries, many could not afford that "luxury." And virtually all of the inmates that responded said they only had access to law libraries for a one-hour session once per week. In addition, most have no access either to the Internet or even to computers. So those men must still write letters and briefs by hand or on typewriters. (One of them sent me a list of items for sale showing that it cost $8.95 just to purchase a typewriter ribbon.)

As to discipline and fighting, the standard response was that during the day at any given moment if an alarm sounded all inmates, whether in the yard or in the dayroom, were required to get down on the ground or prostrate on the floor. The alarm sounds when there is a riot on any of the yards, when an inmate has a heart attack or has overdosed, or if any inmates get into fights. The frequency of these fights and riots depends upon the institution and mostly its racial environment. The norm for most prisons is about two to four fights per week — mostly just between two individuals trying to knock each other out with fists or stab each other with a homemade shiv. The usual causes of fights are disputes over drug or gambling debts not being paid or from allegations of theft. The way mostly to avoid trouble is to respect people, be polite and say you are sorry if you are wrong (pretty much like life on the outside). Solitary confinement is used at most prisons for various rule violations and misconduct. Of course, inmates often state that the guards can sometimes really be petty about its use as a sanction, and probably many times the inmates are right.

As to substance abuse and overdose problems, all responders consistently said that these are huge problems. In that regard, the standard response is that the illicit drug business is primarily dominated by the Mexican Mafia. It is easily observable that an enormous amount of crystal-meth, heroine, fentanyl, tobacco, and

cannabis can be seen daily, both being sold and used around the yard
and in the dayrooms. Hypodermic needles, sold by or stolen from
diabetics after administering their insulin, are sold on the yard for
between $20 to as much as $100 each and are also being shared by
other users. A piece of heroine smaller than a standard pencil eraser
often sells for $50 to $60.

So how is it that these drugs enter the prison yards? It's mostly
not the mail because that most often is heavily scrutinized. Instead the
substances are mostly inserted into a balloon which is, in turn,
inserted into the body cavities of visitors who, after visiting for a
while, go to a bathroom to retrieve it, conceal it in their clothing and
then hand it to the inmate who then swallows it and awaits it to be
retrieved later from his bowl movements. They are also brought in by
free staff, correctional officers and nurses — the same people who also
bring in contraband cell phones. Why? Simple economics. There is
lots of money to be made. For example, a typical $49.95 Wal-Mart cell
phone sells for between $1,000 and $1,200 inside a prison. So it's hard
to resist a 2,000% profit for one day's work. One inmate said that some
of the free staff bring as many as half a dozen phones at a time in the
bottom of their sack lunches, and he estimates that at least 10 percent
of inmates in his yard own cell phones, which are mostly used to
coordinate drug smuggling.

In addition to smuggled drugs it also seems that each prison has
full-time psychiatrists who freely prescribe "mountains" of
psychotropic drugs. There are long lines for these "brain drainers"
three times daily, which often leave inmates with serious mood
swings. According to the inmate correspondents, these drugs are
provided mostly and simply to keep the mentally ill in a docile state
of mind, which makes it easier for the staff to manage them. But an

additional problem is that it is very common for "druggies" to be "celled up" with non-users who are eventually robbed and beaten up by drug users to support their habit. "A very unsafe environment."

Generally, it is understood that there is nothing "correctional" about any of the "correctional facilities." A further theme was that many inmates use their time in prison to plan how not to get caught the next time, which makes prisons quite useful in creating better criminals. But there is a larger group that simply wants to have a better life. So, since it costs about $80,000 per year to keep one inmate confined, it would be highly cost-effective for the taxpayers to provide the means to help inmates from being returned to custody after they are eventually released.

Thus to reduce injustices, harms and expenses to the taxpayers, I believe we must on an institutional and regular basis shine a neutral light upon life inside our prisons. The best way for this to be done is to allow, for example, an association of media outlets to appoint one of its members to have free and regular access to each prison — obviously taking security and safety issues into account. Then those representatives would be free to research and publish stories about whatever they find. But that should be tempered by requiring the media outlets also to publish rejoinders by the prison wardens whenever they so desire.

The United States of America has 5 percent of the world's population, but 25 percent of its prisoners. So, at least in this area "We're Number One!" (Does this make you proud?) So how did this happen? As stated above, beginning in the early 1970s with the so-called War on Drugs, we converted the political slogan of "Tough on Crime" into governmental policy. As a result, today there are literally tens of thousands of people in prison who simply should not be there, and that must be changed. This can be addressed by empowering governmental review boards to determine whether, all things considered, some inmates have served enough time.

In addition, by repealing things like "Three Strikes and You're Out" laws, mandatory minimum sentences and many existing sentencing enhancements, we can re-allow more judicial discretion in sentencing to make the punishments more fit the crimes. Yes, there are some people in our world who see us as their natural prey, and they by rights should be removed from society. But most people should not be defined by the worst thing they have ever done. As a judge, I was in the "Responsibility Business." But I ask you the reader, please close your eyes, right this minute, and contemplate how you would feel if you knew you would be spending the next ten years of your life wasting away behind bars, much less 20 years or 30! Particularly non-violent or first-time offenders! Too many people who are not a threat to us are facing that future, and it should be re-evaluated, on a case by case basis.

A large segment of people in prison are also mentally ill and who are not receiving necessary treatment to address their "demons." That is both inhumane and counterproductive for both the security of those inmates as well as everyone else involved.

It is also a fact that many prison inmates are geriatrics who couldn't hurt anyone even if they tried to throw their walkers at them. In addition, many of these older inmates often are preyed upon by gangs of younger inmates. So, if they cannot be released, then separate lower-security facilities should be set aside for those who are, for example, 55 and older. Not only will this be safer and more humane, it will also be much more cost-effective to gather these older inmates in the same places.

Of critical and humane importance, eligibility for parole must be returned to the federal system! People can change in prison, and those who have become prison role models and otherwise shown they are no longer threats to the rest of us or our property should have a chance to be released before their entire term has been served!

In my November 8, 2019, podcast interview of Mr. Justin Brooks, who is the director of the San Diego "Innocence Project," he told us that he himself in the past 20 years has personally escorted 29 people out of our prisons who were "factually innocent." Even one person in prison who is factually innocent is too many, but 29? Another reason to allow a member of the media to have free access to our prisons!

Inmates should have reasonable access to law libraries, as well as computers and copy machines. Every one of the inmate correspondents brought up this issue, and they have a valid point!

All studies show that the key to not being a repeat offender, i.e. a recidivist, is having a job. So, if only for taxpayer relief, job skills should be taught to those who want them before the inmates are released. Furthermore, since many states require licensing for many trades, such as hair braiding, tree trimming, plumbing, mechanics and even dental and medical assistants, many released inmates are disqualified from even applying for those licenses. This must be changed for many of them!

One example of a successful approach is being implemented by a group called Open Gate International, which provides training in culinary arts without cost not only to inmates who have been released after serving their sentences, but also to some inmates while they are still in prison. And this wonderful group has a 75% success rate in getting good jobs for their graduates as chefs and other similar positions. Just think of the benefits to society that this group obtains! These programs should be replicated!

There is also good news in that there are often work opportunities available inside prisons, such as janitorial, maintenance, plumbing, electrical helpers and general workers at factories inside or even outside some prisons. But, unfortunately, there are also large disincentives for inmates to participate. For example, most say that the wages range between 5 and 16 cents per hour. And further disincentives are found because many inmates have been court-ordered to pay restitution to their various victims. So often 55% of their wages are garnished for those restitution payments, and that often doesn't even cover the interest that is charged for the outstanding balances. "So why should I work?" is often the understandable feeling. Changes should be made to provide more incentives for inmates to work.

Virtually everyone agrees that inmates should not be pampered, but some reasonable air conditioning should be provided in prisons that are located in desert or semi-desert locations. In addition, given the situation, meditation classes would be wonderfully fitted to prison life, where there mostly are no tools available, lots of pent up anger and the inmates have lots of "time" on their hands. These would help everyone to "keep the lid on."

In summary, as a humane society, we must guarantee that anyone who is in our custody is treated with at least a minimum threshold of decency, nutrition, health and dental care and safety. All of the inmate responders brought up examples of an absence of medical and dental care, to the degree that several said that not even Poli-Grip was available in the commissary store for inmates with dentures. That is not humane. Let's all join together and treat those people who are in our custody in a fashion that would assure Dostoevsky and anyone else who cares that walking into our nation's prisons would reflect well upon us as a humane and caring society. Because it appears now that this is not the situation.

Frankly, if we were to modify the way we do business in the criminal justice system, we can reduce government spending. As mentioned, adopting policies of restorative justice, changing away from our country's failed and hopeless policy of Drug Prohibition, coming to terms with the fact that the death penalty as a policy is extremely expensive but is simply not working, and readjusting our thinking and approaches to the problems of juvenile gangs are some of the most important ways in which we can modify our current system. There are also some tools that we should deploy along the way to help people confront and overcome some of their problems, such as drug courts to address addiction, peer courts to teach responsible choices and ethics to juveniles, and community courts to help the homeless and mentally disabled to address their problems.

So what is peer court (also known as youth court or teen court)? We started our peer court in Orange County, California in 1994. The purpose was to provide an institutional means for our young people to focus upon ethics, individual responsibility, the long-range importance in their lives of getting accurate information and making intelligent decisions based upon it, and the fact that they are important role models for others, especially their younger siblings.

Our Peer court is a diversion program that presents real juvenile court cases that are carefully screened by the probation department to high school "jurors." The juvenile subjects must admit the truth of the charged offenses and, along with their parents, waive their rights to confidentiality. Then they personally appear at a high school outside of their own school district (so that no one present knows them) with at least one parent present. Frequently the jurors' questions show, to the astonishment of some parents, that the students actually expect the parents to parent. A sample question might be, "What do you mean that you didn't know your sixteen-year-old daughter was out with friends at 2 AM on a school night?"

The established procedure is for a jury of students at the host high school to be impaneled after some short questioning to determine if they can be fair and impartial. A probation officer reads a statement of facts about the case, and then the subjects can make comments about themselves, their backgrounds, the offenses, or anything they feel would be important for the jury to know about the situation. A sitting county judge presides over each of the sessions, and also asks questions, but the program is designed for most of the questioning to be done by the high school jurors themselves.

For example, the students usually expect the subjects to acknowledge their negative influence on others. They might ask subject questions like: So you were smoking marijuana that evening, correct? And you said you have a younger sister. Don't you agree that you are an important person in her life and that she really looks up to you? Do you want your sister to smoke marijuana? Because if she learns that you smoke marijuana, she probably will think it's the thing to do. Had you thought of that before?" The answer is usually along the lines of, "No, I guess you're right. I really had not thought about that before."

Whenever I was a judge in a peer court, I would use the occasion to reinforce some of society's values that, in many ways, seem to have eroded. For example, before a male subject sits down, I expected him to assist his mother first in taking her seat. And since this is still a real court, it is entitled to the same sanctity that accompanies it: no gum chewing; no talking to one's neighbors while court is in session; no untucked shirttails and the like. Sometimes, I used the opportunity to try and make important points that most young people have not thought of before. For instance, I will stress, "There is no such thing as peer pressure. Each of us is the captain of our own ship, and no one can make us do anything against our will. Do you agree?" I also ask the subjects to think about who their three best friends are. Then, without telling us who they are, I ask them if they feel that these friends will be successful in their lives. The answer is almost always in the negative. So then I tell them a secret: "You show me your friends, and I'll show you your future." If you hang out with "friends" who smoke marijuana, ditch school and talk back to their parents and teachers, you will probably end up doing the same thing. But if you spend time with student who apply themselves and work hard, and who will likely be successful, the same result will probably come your way. Had you thought of that before?

After enough questions are asked to enable to the jurors to feel that they have received sufficient information, the jury retires along with a volunteer adult attorney advisor to deliberate and reach a recommended sentence to the give to the judge. The attorney advisor tries to keep the jury focused but does not participate in the deliberations.

When the jury returns, the judge reviews the recommendations and tries to incorporate them into the sentence. Then if the juvenile subject completes the sentence within four months, the underlying offenses are dismissed. (That is why peer court is called a diversion program.) The only sanction for a failure to complete the sentence is to refer the underlying offense back to the district attorney for prosecution. Obviously, the district attorney must exercise appropriate discretion in making this decision; however, that office has stated that it will consider the subject's failure of the diversion program as a "factor in aggravation" in whether or not to proceed. We stress that these are serious matters. Of course, even though juvenile records are still sealed for most purposes, there are always exceptions and the risks of having a criminal conviction, even as a juvenile, should never be taken lightly.

Some of the other programs around the country use high school "attorneys" to prosecute or defend the cases, and the guilt or innocence of the subjects is determined by high school juries, as well as the sentences if the subjects are "convicted." Some peer courts are held at courthouses and some are held at local high schools, but most often not the high school that the subject attends. Most of the programs of which I am aware have a high school jury that deliberates and then returns with a recommended sentence to a real judge, who tries to impose as much of that sentence as is practical. The sentences can virtually involve anything except incarceration or a fine. Most often they include community service, half of which is picking up trash in a park, and the other half which is served at a fire station, boys' and girls' club, or a comparable venue. Counseling and restitution are required as appropriate and serving as a juror at a future peer court session are also frequently imposed.

The beauty of programs like these is that not only do they keep subjects from having juvenile records, but they also are successful in getting the subjects to start thinking about the choices they make, their actions, and the people whom they "hang out with." And who learns these important lessons? Of course, the focus is upon the subject, but often the parents learn lessons as well. In addition, often the jurors themselves are able to focus upon the lessons and learn from them, as are the approximately 50 students in the audience. So this program almost always gets a valuable bang for the bucks spent, and I am proud of them!

So who wins under a more Libertarian approach to the criminal justice system? Among them are people who are incarcerated or otherwise led astray by our laws of Drug Prohibition, a vast percentage of whom are teenagers or people of color, or both. If marijuana would be strictly regulated and controlled the same way we treat wine, and other presently illicit drugs were to be placed under the care of healthcare professionals, we would strongly reduce the incentives for people to sell these drugs on the illegal market. Another fact you should know is that under today's system many juvenile street gangs use the sale of illicit drugs as a recruiting tool to lure other young people into that practice. And who do juveniles sell illicit drugs to? Other juveniles, thus recruiting more young people into a lifestyle of drug usage and drug selling! This is an unnecessary tragedy. Think of it this way: today it is easier for our young people to obtain marijuana, or any other illicit drugs, if they want to, than it is alcohol. Why is that? Because illicit drug dealers don't ask for ID.

So who loses under Libertarian governance? Prison guard's unions, who often see today's sentencing laws as their golden goose. And, since it is so easy to get into the criminal justice system and hard to get out, many defendants unnecessarily lose their futures because of some mistakes they made at an early age. This also is often an unnecessary tragedy. And that is not even talking about the harm inflicted upon the defendants' families, because not only have they frequently lost a breadwinner, they have also lost the guidance and affection of a loving parent. And, of course, the taxpayers are being punished because prison is almost always the most expensive response to any criminal justice problem. Yes, prisons are and always will be necessary to remove some people from our society who see us as their lawful prey, and even strictly as deserved punishment, but they are presently being vastly overdone in our country. So this must be rethought.

Chapter 5

Liberty and the Economy

In my view, the most dangerous threat to our safety and security is not the possibility of being invaded by another country, or even the terrorist actions of any of the world's radical elements. Instead, the greatest threat facing the safety of our country is a weak national economy. Ancient Greece, Ancient Rome, and the Ottoman Empire were really not conquered by external forces. Instead, they overspent themselves to death and spread themselves too thin. That is a major lesson in history, and the Government of the United States of America has not learned that lesson. All unproductive expenditures of the federal government must be eliminated, as a matter of our nation's security!

How can this be done? Well, we as taxpayers and voters must demand that our government return to financial responsibility: in every respect, big and small. For example, I received a really expensive brochure "Report to the District" from my congressman some years ago — naturally prepared at taxpayer expense. (You probably have received some of those as well.) Okay, fine. All congressional representatives do it. But that is no excuse. It had to have cost a lot of taxpayer money. So I sent him a letter and suggested that, if such a report was necessary at all, it be provided in the form of a simple and inexpensive letter. To his credit he wrote back personally and said that I would never again see such a mailing from him. (I took this as a positive sign, but maybe that means I was simply taken off his mailing list.)

Fundamentally, it is up to us all to monitor all of our government's spending. Every line item in our federal budget must be scrutinized as publicly as possible, and the size of the federal bureaucracy must be reduced. This will materially reduce government spending. People must understand that government does not in itself produce wealth. Instead it detracts from it by taking wealth from others. We can and must do better. We can regain our economic strength without withdrawing from our military and other obligations. But we must have a change in thinking and a change in approach. And it begins with us. You and I must cause that change to take place.

There is a story that, at the close of our Constitutional Convention, Benjamin Franklin was asked what type of government the delegates had agreed upon for our country. He was heard to respond: "A Republic, if you can keep it." Our Founders established for us a government ruled by law but based upon the individual "We the People" as the sovereigns. But each of us must do our part. If we don't vote and oversee government, the special interests will. Likewise, if we don't monitor and mentor our children, and provide them with productive visions of the future, they will be more likely be mentored by drug dealers, juvenile street gangs and other thugs and thus unnecessarily become unproductive and antisocial. And in a similar fashion, if we are not vigilant, we could lose our cherished Republic.

So as to our financial situation today, we are certainly facing daunting challenges. Naturally, it is important for our general feelings of economic confidence to believe that government is "doing something" positive about the situation. But this also brings upon us the risk that we, and the government, will see government as the solution to all of our problems. And, ask people like John Locke and Adam Smith, that is a dangerous course to take for our future, and for the future of our children. So, let me walk you through the Libertarian way of strengthening our economy.

Simply put, there are four ways to spend money. The first is that you can spend your own money on yourself. That will be done carefully, and you probably will get your money's worth. The second is you can spend your money on someone else. There you will mostly get your money's worth, but you will be careful not to spend too much. The third is you can spend someone else's money on yourself. There you will probably get fairly good deals on things you mostly do not need. And fourth, you can spend someone else's money on someone else. There you will get what we see in our nation's troubled but expensive government school system.

Sheldon Richman, the former editor of *The Freeman* and the executive editor of *The Libertarian Institute*, published a book in 1999 called *Abolish the Income Tax*. In that work Richman discusses how we have spawned such an expensive and intrusive federal government, and what it does to repress Liberty. Though some time has passed since it was hot off the press, it is still extremely informative and relevant, particularly to illustrate the fourth way of spending money. He refers to this as "the transfer state," and goes on to explain that "Social Security imposes taxes on working people and hands the money to retired people. Medicare does almost the same thing, except the money goes to doctors and hospitals. Agricultural programs take money from taxpayers and consumers and give it to farmers for growing or even not growing particular crops. Welfare programs give the taxpayers' money to people who do not work. Subsidies reward well-connected business people with the hard-earned money of the middle and working classes. Foreign aid indirectly subsidizes particular American businesses by giving tax money to foreign governments that will buy American products and services. Government cultural agencies transfer wealth to artists, musicians, broadcasters, and humanities scholars. The education bureaucracy subsidizes teachers' unions and trendy social experiments on children. The defense bureaucracy floods contractors with cash for equipment that often is not needed and for missions that are improper."

Alexis de Tocqueville, after his famous tour of the United States in 1831, drew attention to this problem when he said that people are constantly excited by two conflicting passions: they want to be led, and they wish to remain free. So people strive to satisfy them both at once, and that leads to irresolvable problems. Then, it's important to say again, de Tocqueville went on to anticipate the time that democracy would eventually collapse. He said that would occur when the people's elected officials finally learned that they could bribe the people into voting for them with the people's own money. We are close to that situation today. It is time for us both to be aware of this fact, and to take action to assure that situation is strongly reduced. How can this be done? First by understanding that government is not the answer to our problems. In fact, as stated by President Ronald Reagan, in many ways government really is the problem because it tends to destroy private initiative.

Let me ask you a few of Milton Friedman's questions: "Why do you believe that political self-interest works better than economic self-interest?" Or, why do you believe that government bureaucrats can make more rational choices for you than you can?

When will we find these governmental "angels of the public good" to better organize our society? And why haven't we found them yet? The plain reality is that all societies run on greed, but the prosperous societies run on individuals that run on their personal interests. Competition under a fair and foreseeable justice system pushes us to advance and, once again, this brings much more creativity and prosperity.

Yes, we as citizens and voters actually have to consider economics, because this is the Invisible Hand that in so many ways drives our decision-making process and that of our great nation. The concept of the Invisible Hand is cleverly explained by Leonard Read in his essay, "I Pencil." It was first published in 1958, and it provides a first-person account of how a pencil is manufactured first by harvesting and then refining the raw materials of cedar, lacquer, graphite, ferrule, factice, pumice, wax and glue, and then assembling them into a pencil. Obviously large numbers of people are involved in this process, including the person who sweeps out the factories and the lighthouse keeper who guides the shipments into port. But none of those workers are directed or forced to cooperate. They do so because of the Invisible Hand of working for their own economic benefit.

Ayn Rand described this phenomenon by saying that "Greed is good!" Unfortunately, that comment has been widely misconstrued, and Libertarians have thus been tarred for generations as approving of greedy people — which is a totally different concept. Instead this means that, to the degree possible, creative energies should be left uninhibited so they can be productively harnessed — for the benefit of the actor, and of us all. Or, as Leonard Read encouraged us, "Have faith that free men and women will respond to the Invisible Hand. This faith will be confirmed."

In order to facilitate this process, the basis for our prosperity is simple: the principle of "choice," or as Milton and his wife Rose Friedman put it in the title of the economic bible they wrote, we must be Free to Choose. What does that mean? It means that the foundations of prosperity that are based upon our free choice are private property rights, a fair and foreseeable system of justice, and entrepreneurship and all of the calculated economic risk-taking that this entails.

I know that this sounds like intellectual egg-head talk, but it really is not. It simply means that we must set up a system that maximizes ways people can choose for themselves how to work and spend their money, instead of having the government make those choices for them. This necessarily means that people will benefit from the good choices they make and be responsible for poor ones. But that is the way to prosperity. Therefore, every time the government substitutes its "wisdom" for ours, it is taking us farther away from prosperity.

For example, if you feel you get good value for your money by having a particular person cut your hair, why should the government require a license before that chosen person can perform that service for you? Remember, if the work is not worth the money charged, the would-be barber will go out of business regardless of what the government license says, and we can always require that these workers be bonded, which will add further protections. Of course, we will still need things like protections against environmental pollution and recourse for defective or even harmful products. But, fortunately, the justice system can handle those issues in most situations.

In the first two summers when I was in college, I worked for a pipeline construction company, mostly painting heavy equipment but also doing a fair amount of pick-up and delivery driving. On one occasion I was picking up something from a hardware store when I noticed a product on their check-out counter. This product came in little plastic bags that would apply cement to wood screws as they were being installed. In my wisdom, since I noticed the charge was five cents a bag, I told the shopkeeper that they should simply give the bags away because the small price wouldn't justify the expense of the accounting. He told me that they had tried that approach, and that their customers would take handfuls of the product when they checked out. But when they later returned and were asked how they liked the product virtually nobody had tried it. However, when people had to pay even as little as five cents, they would mostly purchase just a few packages, but when they later returned they mostly said they had used and really liked the product. My lesson: if someone has to pay for a product, they will take it seriously, regardless of the even small amount paid. In other words, they have "skin in the game." It is a lesson I have never forgotten, and it applies almost universally.

So where do taxes fit in? Empirical research has found that throughout history large cuts in taxes and government spending have directly resulted in substantial increases in investment and entrepreneurship. Botswana, for example, in a short time progressed from one of Africa's poorest nations into one of middle-range income after cutting taxes. Similar effects were fairly recently observed in Ireland and New Zealand. The truth is that, again citing Milton

Friedman, no people have broken away from poverty except under a system of capitalism and free trade, and that means free economic choice. The big problems come when foreign aid and government interference undercut the local entrepreneurship.

Similarly, our efforts at foreign aid would be ever much more successful in non-emergency situations if we would make small business loans of money or even farm animals to the people at the bottom of the economic ladder, instead of providing loans of money and products directly to foreign governments. The former are used by the people to set up and expand local businesses, which create prosperity, and the latter are most often used by politicians to purchase expensive automobiles and set up in Swiss bank accounts.

As Anne Frank wrote in her diary, which became a literary classic, "A quiet conscience makes one strong." She is right. We need that quiet conscience now. We must rely on ourselves and our innate abilities and ethics to overcome our problems of today. And we must not give in to the false but seductive allure that the answer lies with the all-knowing and all-protective government. Instead we should remember the saying: "If it's to be, it's up to me."

So how do property rights fit into this discussion, and why are they so important in producing a thriving economy? Part of the answer is explained by the theory of the Tragedy of the Commons. Let me give you an example. Consider that there was a grove of apple trees growing wild somewhere along the Oregon Trail during the covered wagon days. So when a wagon train would come upon it, the travelers would pick more of the ripe apples than they needed. And, why not? They're free! Then the people in the next train would probably pick all of the remaining ripe apples, and most of the green ones as well. Why not? They're free, and the travelers can always feed the unripe apples to their oxen. So soon there would be no more apples at all on the trees. But the people in the next train would cut down the branches and even the trunks of the trees to use as firewood. Why not? They can use the wood, and if they don't cut it down, someone else behind them will.

Therefore, in this situation, not only would no one plant, feed and prune the trees and harvest the apples for maximum benefit, the trees would actually be plundered and soon destroyed. That is the Tragedy of the Commons. Instead of being husbanded and protected, the apples, the trees, the fish in the ocean, the water in the rivers and the minerals in the earth, all will be plundered, "because if we don't someone else will." But if a private person had enforceable ownership rights to the apple grove, enforced by a fair and foreseeable system of justice, there would very likely be an abundance of apples for everyone. The owner of the apple trees would price them at a competitive rate, so the people in the first wagon train would only purchase what they really needed. Of course, then apples would also be available for the later wagons. In other words, with enforceable property rights, people have the incentive to work hard and plan for the long run future because they will profit from their efforts. But without those property rights, the incentives instead are for people to plunder the resources in the short run before someone else does so.

Now to take this discussion one step further, let me ask you a question. Who has more incentive to plant, organize and develop a better apple grove, private people working for their own self-interest, or the government? For the answer to that question, ask the people of Poland, the Czech Republic, or Cuba. Or compare the productivity level of South as opposed to North Korea, or previously West Germany as opposed to East Germany. Furthermore, what is a better way to decide how many washing machines to manufacture, or how many black cars to produce instead of red cars? To have a government bureaucrat make the decision, or a private company that is sensitive to the free market choices of its customers?

To have a system of government decisions in the marketplace leads to what Dr. Milton Friedman calls the "tyranny of control." And bureaucrats always have a natural tendency to increase their power and their area of influence. That is a major explanation for our government being so large, controlling and wasteful today. But to have the decisions made privately brings the most rational decisions in manufacturing and distribution. And that brings prosperity!

Of course, there is a need for a federal government, but that need is generally just for a strong military, national court system and police network, system of currency, and matters of foreign relations. For other government roles we should go back to the concept of Federalism — which made our country great! That means that the most local government that is able effectively to address a particular issue would have the authority and power to do so. Finally, as it states in both the 9th and 10th Amendments to the U.S. Constitution, unless powers are expressly delegated by the Constitution to the federal government, all of the remaining powers should be reserved for states and the people themselves.

Again as a result of my research for a musical, I wrote about the 1787 Constitutional Convention, I have become quite familiar with the beliefs of our Founders. And one of those beliefs, which was enshrined in Article I, sections 9 and 10 of our Constitution, was that there would be no tariffs imposed on trade between or among the states. Can you imagine the harmful effect it would have had if, for example, Virginia had been able to have imposed tariffs for goods it imported from Maryland? Such tariffs would have been deeply destructive to our nation's economy. As a result, Virginia, Maryland and all of the other states since that time have been able to focus upon what they did best, and also derive the benefit of receiving goods and services from other states that were derived from what they did best as well. And this accrued to everyone's benefit.

But today, it is far easier for businesses in our country to trade with China, India, Germany, or any other country than it was for Maryland to trade with Virginia in the 18th Century. And trade barriers among countries have the same effect as they would have had among our states. So let China, Mexico, Japan and Indonesia focus upon what they do best, and let our consumers here benefit by being able to purchase high quality products for reasonable competitive prices from those countries. All the while the businesses in our country will be able to focus upon what they do best, with the same result. And, besides, this will also bring numerous other additional benefits. For example, countries have a deep tendency not to go to war with their customers, so this will reduce military strife. And if the people in Mexico, Guatemala and Indonesia are better able to profit from producing goods in their own countries, their economy will be stronger, with the result that not so many people will feel the necessity to emigrate from their country to ours. So, once again, Liberty works!

China still has government control over many manufacturing businesses, but has been increasingly successful since the death of Mao Zedong in allowing individuals within the companies to make those business decisions. Otherwise, virtually every other place that has ever tried to have manufacturing and pricing decisions made by central planners has ended up in misery, if not starvation. So why do we not celebrate the Free Market System more fully and broadly? Because people like us tend to be quiet when other people who get carried away by emotion sing the praises of Socialism. And when they do they literally do not know what they are talking about.

With smaller, more cost-effective governments, taxes would be reduced, and people would retain more of their money to spend and invest, all of which would further spur the economy for everybody. Thomas Jefferson famously said that we should have a bloody revolution every generation to keep the vested interests at bay. Well, our Constitution can keep it from being bloody, but how long has it been since we had a revolution? The late 1850s, when the Republicans took over from the Whigs? So maybe it's long since time for a revolution to take place! And the Libertarian Party is the only hope in sight!

Chapter 6

Liberty and Healthcare

P.J. O'Rourke stated it best when he said that if you think healthcare is expensive now, wait until it's free. If we keep going in the same direction we have been for the last twenty years we will be heading for a healthcare disaster. And the evidence of our failing healthcare system is all around us. Costs are out of control, emergency rooms and entire hospitals are going out of business, competent doctors and other healthcare providers are getting out of the profession, and there are allegations that poor people who are sick are being "dumped" back onto the streets. How and why has this happened?

The answer to that critical question can be traced directly back to the federal government increasingly taking control of the system. Before the mid-1960s, the United States had one of the best healthcare systems in the world, both with regard to the quality of goods and services and the relatively low cost. But slowly the government started taking control of the system, with demonstrably disastrous results.

As we have traveled more deeply into socialized medicine, we see that it is the administrators instead of the healthcare professionals who have received greater financial benefits. If we want our healthcare to be run by the equivalent of the Department of Motor Vehicles instead of a coalition between us and our healthcare professionals, we are well on our way toward that end. For example, in the United Kingdom, where the government runs the healthcare system, some officials are now proposing that, since obesity is a health problem, the government should start restricting the number of calories that people would be allowed to ingest each day. Imagine the costs and intrusions into our lives of monitoring and enforcing such a scheme. But this, of course, would be a logical result, because when governments have a financial interest in our health, they have an economic incentive to micromanage our lives.

And if we were to implement programs of "Medicare for All," which would "guarantee" health insurance as a "right" for all, Libertarians understand that private health insurance would soon vanish and taxes would soon be severely increased. Furthermore, what people really want and need is not medical insurance, it is medical coverage! What good is medical insurance if no competent healthcare professionals will accept it because their compensation is being continually reduced? In addition, with a healthcare system based upon government control instead of competition, medical care would become more restricted in the form of delayed testing and treatment, which is the result of the present Canadian system. Why is that? Because if there is no economic incentive for healthcare professionals to profit from providing increased services, not only will they cut back on those services, fewer people will want to go through all of the schooling and training required to enter the profession in the first place. Accordingly, under the Libertarian system of competition, other than the government funding a system of vouchers issued on a sliding scale based upon economic earnings that could be used to pay for healthcare insurance and co-pays, the government would no longer be involved. This will result in both healthcare professionals and their patients coming out much farther ahead. And, overriding all of this, it simply is the right thing to do.

Since 1980, the costs of medical care have quadrupled in the United States, even taking inflation into account. How and why has this happened? That is an easy question to answer. As the costs of prescriptions, treatment, screenings, testing, and simple doctor visits have become less transparent, they have risen enormously. And how has this come about? It began during World War II, when the wages that employers could pay their employees was frozen. So how could employers entice more skilled and able employees to work for them if they couldn't increase their salaries? The answer was to offer the employees benefits like medical insurance that were provided in addition to their wages. And this situation was compounded again under President Nixon's system of wage and price controls. So now, as we know, a large percentage of employees have their health insurance paid for by their employers.

How has that raised prices? Again, an easy question to answer. Today, for example, if people covered by health insurance see their doctor about a knee problem and the doctor asks them if they want to have an MRI, what goes through the patients' minds? " Well, I have health insurance, and the co-pay for me will only be about $30, so why not? I might as well get the best." But if those patients actually paid their own money for the MRI, what would they be asking? "Okay Doc, what will the MRI show us and how much will it cost?" But today, unfortunately, cost is not even a factor, to the extent that most of the time the doctors don't even know what the cost is. So that is naturally why the costs have skyrocketed.

How can we bring them down? Bring in Liberty, which will have patients pay for their own healthcare. That will not only make the patients larger partners with their doctors in their own healthcare, but it will bring in competition back into healthcare, with the easily foreseeable results of lower competitive prices.

For example, consider the areas of medical practice still in effect today in which patients receive quality care and services at competitive prices. What are they? Lasik eye surgery and cosmetic surgery. Why? Because those procedures are subject to the free market and are not restricted by governmental or even insurance control. As a result, most magazines, newspapers and other media are filled with advertisements from various doctors who have "done this procedure thousands of times," and who will provide the same quality service to you at low cost and easy monthly payments, etc.

How can we take advantage of market competition in the healthcare field? It's not that hard. Just bring in a system of medical savings accounts for those of us who can take care of our own medical needs and combine it with a system of vouchers on a sliding scale that will address the medical needs of those who are not so financially secure. In fact, since this is important, let's dive in a little deeper.

To reduce the involvement of government for people who are able to take care of their own healthcare needs, I propose a simple requirement of $5,000 per person invested yearly into a Medical Savings Account. This strategy is based upon two timeless truths. The first is that people get the best results at the greatest value when they spend their own money upon themselves, which is Milton Friedman's first scenario. And the second is that the best healthcare results also occur when patients become active partners with their healthcare professional in addressing their own healthcare needs. A Medical

Savings Account would be a separate ATM-type account that they would use to pay for their own healthcare needs. In addition, they would be required to purchase catastrophic healthcare insurance, which would basically be insurance with a $5,000 deductible. Research shows that most people spend less than $5,000 per year for their healthcare needs until reaching the latter years of their lives. So if they have an incentive to spend their money wisely, and know that the remaining amount will be rolled over into the next year's account and eventually be available for their retirements, they will do just that.

This program will produce at least three beneficial results. The first would be to increase competition for healthcare dollars, which will bring down those costs. The second would be that the amount of money paid to healthcare professionals would be materially increased, and the amount paid to administrators and bureaucrats materially decreased. And the third would be once again to encourage people more to act as active partners with their healthcare professionals in their own health. All of these are good results.

But what about people who are not able financially to take care of their own needs? They would be provided with government-paid vouchers which could be used by them to pay for their own healthcare needs as well as insurance. These vouchers would be provided on a sliding scale based upon each person's financial condition, but there would always be some form of co-pay, however slight, to encourage responsible purchases. This approach would then furnish the same basic results as set forth above. Thus everyone would be encouraged to spend their money/vouchers productively thus bringing costs down. And this approach would also remove inequitable tax breaks for employer-based insurance plans and encourage everyone to act as partners in their own healthcare. So, what's not to like?

There's also another way to increase the quality of healthcare in our country while lowering the costs. How? By allowing pharmacists to provide certain medications that are presently prescription-only, i.e., which require a visit to a physician. In that regard, the United States is one of only a few developed countries in the world that divides drugs into only two strict categories: "prescription only" and "over-the-counter." Many other countries, such as Australia, Canada, and many countries in Europe, also have a third category, which is "behind the counter." This category of drugs can be provided to an adult without a prescription, but only after a consultation with a licensed pharmacist.

In today's healthcare world, the talents of licensed pharmacists are vastly under-utilized. This is extremely wasteful because licensed pharmacists generally are better schooled in the effects, risks and benefits of drugs and combinations of drugs than most physicians. So why should patients be forced to take the time and pay the cost to visit a physician for advice and a prescription for drugs in more routine cases when pharmacists generally have more information and actually specialize in this area? And why must the patient repeat the process 12 months later (if not more often, for some prescriptions) for a refill on the same prescription if it is working?

To be licensed, pharmacists must complete a minimum of five years in college, but most even extend for a sixth year for a Doctor of Pharmacy degree. In addition, they must pass a national standardized licensing examination, a practical exam and also an individual state pharmacy law test. And after they are licensed, they must be bonded and obtain continuing educational credits for the renewal of their licenses.

There are two main reasons why pharmacists do not give independent professional advice about the risks and benefits of drugs and drug combinations. One, pharmacists do not diagnose diseases and potential remedies. Two, their advice might conceivably contravene with that of the physicians. Therefore, it is often argued, to allow pharmacists to provide behind-the-counter drugs to patients directly would interfere with the relationship between physician and patient. But often the patients already know what they need, and if the pharmacists have any questions, they can always refer the patients to their doctors. With regard to the possible interference with the doctor-patient relationship, under the quality of today's "managed healthcare," the amount of time that most physicians are able to spend with their patients for either medication selection or an explanation of the risks and benefits of the medications has been seriously reduced. So both of these objections have lost much of their validity.

Accordingly, our laws and regulations should be changed in two important ways. The first is to allow adults to be able to obtain some drugs like birth-control pills, cholesterol, and migraine medications, and all-other prescription drugs, except those that are addictive or in the penicillin family. Second, before any such drug could be provided, the pharmacist would have to consult directly with the patient and refer to the patient's drug history chart, which would be stored electronically. For privacy reasons, only the patient would have the password to give access to the pharmacists. But once a medication was provided, the drug history chart would be updated to reflect that fact. Of course, matters of cybersecurity and privacy will certainly pose a risk, but it isn't one that has stopped us from converting to paper-free record-keeping and bureaucracy in recent years.

What would the results of this program be? Just like in the countries mentioned above, patients would have access to appropriate medications at greatly reduced costs. But far from receiving their medication "from a vending machine," the professional pharmacists would probably be providing more expert and individually tailored advice than patients are generally receiving today.

A discussion of other benefits would be addressed by asking the following question: who has the most to lose by an overdose or misdiagnosis of medications? Obviously, the answer is the patient. As a result, patients would again increasingly have the incentive to become more educated about their own conditions instead of blindly following the advice of their overworked and underpaid physicians. That would, in turn, shift the relationship between physician and patient from one of paternalism to one of partnership.

In fact, efforts to expand birth control access have resulted in several states adopting a new policy allowing pharmacists to prescribe hormonal birth control products, such as pills, patches, injections, and vaginal rings. At the fury of OB-GYNs, you wonder? To the contrary! Those at the forefront of the efforts to expand access to birth control are often many OB-GYNs themselves. Today, women in California, Oregon, Washington, Utah, Colorado, New Mexico, Tennessee, Maryland, and New Hampshire have accessible family planning options. As discussed in this book's chapter "Liberty and Our Children," the percentage of pregnancies that were to unwed mothers is 39.6, but what about unintended pregnancies? In the U.S., the rate of unintended pregnancies is, optimistically, at an all-time low of 45 percent.

That's far from low. Plenty of research has indicated the economic and educational attainment limitations such a situation creates for many women. Let's take the state of Colorado, for example. Since 2009, when they began implemented their family planning initiative, their abortion rates and teen pregnancy rates have more than halved. These astounding results have logically caught the eyes of other policy makers.' (Again we must applaud the benefits of the concept of Federalism!) So a prescribing pharmacist may not be too far-fetched a course to take in the near future.

There's another change that will reduce the costs of effective healthcare while increasing the general fairness of the healthcare system. Expanding the scope of "direct access" for physical therapy across the United States. Before I detail this concept, I must tell you that my wife is a physical therapist who formerly owned and managed her own physical therapy practice in the City of Orange. So, maybe I have a bias.

But direct access refers to a patient's ability to seek physical therapy directly without needing a physician's prescription or referral. What does that mean? Today, patients who are covered by health insurance can go for evaluation and treatment directly to their chosen chiropractor, acupuncturist, marriage and family counselor, or psychologist and have those visits reimbursed by their health insurers without being first required to obtain a prescription from a physician. But to go see a physical therapist, in many states, you must first obtain that prescription. This, of course, requires patients to spend extra time and money before they can obtain their physical therapy.

How did this disparity occur? Probably due to its weak or dormant political lobby and its relative youth as a recognized profession. The evolution of physical therapy in the United States accelerated due to the major wars of the 20th century. Many soldiers that returned with injuries and disabilities needed physical therapy as a part of their recovery. Thus physical therapists created educational and training programs to educate and employ more of them to meet rising demands. In 1965, then California's Attorney General Thomas Lynch issued an opinion that interpreted the legislative intent of the Physical Therapy Practice Act to require access to a physical therapist only after a prescription from a physician. This opinion was rendered even though it was and still is contrary to the protocol of Medicare and many managed-care health plans.

Currently, twenty states have unrestricted direct access policies. The remaining states either have direct access policies with provisions giving access to evaluation and treatment, but with stipulations on time or visit limit, or referral requirements for uncommon treatments, or limited patient access, meaning that only some patient populations in particular circumstances may receive limited treatment. The American Physical Therapy Association (APTA) speaks for the profession, and their vision is to expand direct access to all states, without those provisions those remaining states are holding on to.

The need for widespread access to physical therapy has always existed, but even more so today. The opioid crisis in the U.S. is strong evidence that pain-management strategies need to change. Prescriptions and sales of opium-derived painkillers quadrupled since 1999. In 2014, when the prescription craze hit its peak, U.S. doctors wrote more than two-hundred and fifty million prescriptions for opioids. Physical therapy is one of the ways in which the underlying causes of some patients' pain can be treated. In 2016, the U.S. Centers for Disease Control and Prevention issued new guidelines hoping to slow down the rate of overdose deaths. For pain management, the CDC urged physicians to refer the patient to a physical therapist, in combination with exercise and over-the-counter medication. To bolden the value of this profession, a study by Seattle's Virginia Mason Medical Center found that putting "physical therapy in front" when treating patients with back pain generally resulted in less waiting for appointments, fewer MRIs and a decrease in time lost from work by the patients. Conservative physical therapy treatment not only is less invasive and less expensive, it often works better than other approaches.

To become licensed, physical therapists must graduate from a physical therapy program accredited through the Commission on Accreditation for Physical Therapy Education. Since January 2003, only physical therapists who have obtained a master's or doctorate can even be considered for that accreditation. Of course, if any healthcare professionals determine that a patient has symptoms or conditions that are outside their field of expertise, they must refer the patient to the appropriate medical specialist. Otherwise, just like in any other profession, the patients/consumers should be able to choose which healthcare professional to see and trust for their evaluation and treatment.

Thus, direct access is a commonsense approach to healthcare delivery that will save patients time and bother, eliminate the burdens and costs of unnecessary visits to physicians, and often lead to quicker pain relief and recovery from injuries when they need them most. Along the way, it will also provide for more basic fairness in the healthcare field.

Another place where lobbyists have been successful has been in requiring customers to get a new eye test before receiving new eyeglasses or contact lenses if their prescription is more than a year old. This is not even a matter health. Libertarians would let the customers decide if their vision is such that they should be tested. But, of course, this is just a way that vested interests have been able to change the laws and regulations for their benefit, instead of the consumers.

But healthcare is a particularly pressing issue in light of the ongoing coronavirus pandemic. The topic of health dramatically pivoted from being a private matter to one of public concern practically overnight. But what have those in power accomplished? By ordering businesses to close and confining citizens to their homes, First and Fifth Amendment rights have been determined, for the time being(?), "non-essential." In the meantime, our government is spending trillions, printing money, and exacerbating a tremendous amount of national debt. The federal response to COVID-19 has underscored a sentiment Libertarians have asserted for a long time: governments cannot centrally plan.

Benjamin Powell, a Professor of Economics at Texas Tech University, authored an Op-Ed piece that was published in the May 3, 2020, edition of the Orange County Register. The article discusses the realities of the attempts by governments to be central planners and to decide when and how to "re-open" our economy. He writes: "Centrally planned economies have a 100-year history of stagnation, inefficiency, and shortages of basic consumer goods. It didn't take a global health crisis to empty the shelves in Cuban or Venezuelan grocery stores. Mistakes made by central planners, who hold monopoly money over economic decisions, did that all on their own." Here in the U.S., the health care sector is one of the most regulated in the economy. As a result, Powell points out that "government planners limit the ability of entrepreneurs to discover better ways of providing health care—with predictable dismal results."

Professor Powell goes on to say that the Centers for Disease Control and the Food and Drug Administration first used their monopoly powers to obstruct private efforts to produce testing for the virus, developing vaccines and bringing new products to market by prohibiting doctors, patients, and entrepreneurial companies from exercising their "right to try." And, yes, finally some progress was made when the CDC provided special "fast-track" approvals to the private sector, but the need for those special approvals simply highlights the problems in central planning, which is: There is a better way.

That way is to employ a system where individuals and entrepreneurs are free to choose how to interact with other businesses and their customers and employees. No one wants to get sick, so employees and customers will be much less likely to work for or frequent businesses where the health risks are too high. But the best solutions will not be the same everywhere because one size, clearly, does not fit all. Instead, the solutions come from the Invisible Hand of the pricing system, economic incentives to make the right decisions and everyone's desire to be and remain healthy. Thus, no government planner can know better than the private sector regarding how to re-open and maintain the economy.

My own observations are that politicians naturally respond to problems by protecting themselves politically. So virtually every governor and mayor said things like "I'm going to do everything in my power to keep you healthy." Why did they do that? Because if you stay healthy: "See, it worked! I am a hero!" And if you did get sick: "Well, you can't blame me because I did everything I could!" Of course, this pandemic brought us serious health issues and of course no one wants to get sick. But government central planners have in the past brought global starvation to millions of people. In addition, the arbitrary closing of hundreds of thousands of "non-essential" businesses and putting literally tens of millions of people out of work also caused more than economic damages: think suicides, depression, and even domestic violence. Politicians with political courage, such as Libertarians, would have left the operations of businesses up to the business owners and their employees and customers.

So, what would the COVID-19 pandemic have looked like with a Libertarian government? In the first place, the government would have been prepared and made plans for emergencies in advance. That is one responsibility of government, and our governments failed badly. Of course, no one can know what, when, or where emergencies might strike, be they earthquakes, hurricanes, or pandemics. But if we don't have plans in place when they do occur, it is too late. That is what we recently experienced with COVID-19. Next, federal agencies like the FDA and CDC would have already had their regulations streamlined so that the free enterprise system could have been able to respond to the emergency — which is what the free enterprise system is best equipped to do. But instead, although about 50 companies had testing kits ready to be marketed, only two were originally approved by the FDA. Similarly, although many companies were ready to manufacture ventilators, they were prohibited from doing so because no permits had been issued. A few valuable lost weeks later the processes for permitting were "fast-tracked," but that only proves that the regulations foster unnecessary delays and should not have been there in the first place.

And then, like was said above, the politicians acted to protect themselves politically, and few politicians demonstrated Libertarian courage. Many, like New York Governor Cuomo, made misguided comments like "If the shutdown saves even one life, it will be worth it," which were transparently pandering to the voters.

Even if you agree that being quarantined and ordered to wear a mask in public by the government are good ideas, what if next time you don't? It is a fact of life that once governments gain power and control over "We the People" they almost never give it up. Of course, in situations like the COVID-19, governments can fill some positive roles in gathering and disseminating accurate information and making recommendations about how we best can remain healthy. But we should never allow governments to keep us in "jail" in our homes without the due process of law for each one of us on an individual basis.

What would have been the Libertarian response? Let individual shop and business owners make adjustments and then advertise them. For example, "Please continue to come to my clothing or hardware store. We have installed a new air filtration system that removes 98.7% of all particles from the air every 30 minutes. We require all who enter, whether employees or customers, to wear masks and to socially distance themselves. We are a small store, so we only allow ten customers to be inside at any one time. And we will have an employee at the door taking the temperature non-invasively of all who enter, and no one with a temperature above 99.4 will be allowed to come in," etc. Then let the customers and employees decide using a risk/gain analysis which responsibly keeps in mind external risks to themselves and others. If the customers are healthy, most will likely continue to shop at those stores, but if they are 80 years old with diabetes or pneumonia, they will almost certainly choose to stay away. The same approach should be taken by places of worship.

On the other hand, government approaches to decide which stores are "non-essential" are arbitrary by their very nature. And, naturally, when many of those small stores are closed down it directly results in customers going to large "essential" box stores where they could buy lots of products, including clothing and hardware. So not only did government close the small stores and help their large competitors, it also put into effect a program that probably exposed the customers to greater risks by placing them into an environment with larger groups of people.

So, once again, the bottom line is that governments cannot centrally plan an economy, and certainly cannot effectively "re-open" one. That can only be done in a Libertarian system where myriads of small decisions are made quickly by both buyers and sellers. If the sellers make good choices, they profit from them. But if they make poor ones, they quickly start losing their market share. And if that happens, they quickly look around at their successful competitors and adjust accordingly. Governments, on the other hand, act in arbitrary fashions, as we have seen. No, Libertarians might be misunderstood because they often go against the "common wisdom," and are not elected because they don't project or protect themselves politically, but Libertarian courage would have vastly reduced the damages that have been and still are being caused by COVID-19.

Chapter 7

School Choice: Liberty and Education

It is no secret that too many public schools today are failing their students. And, tragically, those who are most affected are in lower economic areas, often involving People of Color. This result is frequently not caused by a lack of funding because, as stated above, many of those failing schools, such as those in the District of Columbia, are among the highest funded public schools in the country. Instead, the failures result from a lack of competition.

And what is the solution? Empower parents to choose where and how the government money will be spent for the education of their children. If a school is not teaching its students well, their parents will have the ability to transfer them to a school that would. And the result? Parents would choose excellence. So this will result in students coming out ahead, as well as good teachers, because they will be in greater demand, and paid accordingly.

Did you know that school choice in the United States isn't all that novel of an idea? Its roots can be traced all the way back to American society in its infancy, where parents selected a school based on location, religious tradition and educational philosophy. There were, however, a substantial number of Catholic immigrants who wanted their children to be educated in lockstep with Catholic religious traditions. So they were able to create a system of privately-funded Catholic schools to fulfill this need.

The modern context for school choice begins with Brown v. Board of Education, a landmark case decided by the U.S. Supreme Court in 1954, that demanded increased choice and quality schools for all students. The movement regained momentum when Dr. Milton Friedman advocated for a school voucher system. In fact, the first time I met Dr. Friedman, I heard him talking about the failures of our "government schools" during a recess in a drug policy forum I was holding in 1993. He called them government schools because they are run as virtual monopolies by the government. Instead, Dr. Friedman suggested a system of vouchers, in which parents could spend the money that the government allotted for the education of their children at whatever school they chose. Well before Friedman's lifetime, John Stuart Mill held the same sentiment, advocating for educational voucher programs in the 19th century.

In the fifth chapter of his book, *On Liberty*, Mill argues that "Were the duty of enforcing universal education once admitted, there would be an end to the difficulties about what the State should teach, and how it should teach, which now convert the subject into a mere battle-field for sects and parties, causing the time and labor which should have been spent in educating to be wasted in quarrelling about education. If the government would make up its mind to require for every child a good education, it might save itself the trouble of providing one."

The distinction between requiring and providing is particularly relevant when examining recent attempts by the federal government to have a hand in education reform. But John Stuart Mill went a bit further, stating that if "the education of the people should be in State hands, I go as far as anyone in deprecating. All that has been said of the importance of the individuality of character, and diversity of opinions and modes of conduct, involves, as of the same unspeakable importance, diversity of education." Some say that John Stuart Mill was ahead of his time, but what if we turned that around and ask, why didn't we listen? In fact, K-12 education vouchers have been around in our country since the 19th century in Maine and Vermont. Suffice it to say, a lot of time has passed since then. But here we are as a nation, centuries later, still grappling with this very issue.

The need for education reform is hardly exclusive to the United States. Our entire planet is filled with countries, communities, and individuals who are making impressive leaps toward advancing education. Africa, the Middle East, and South Asia are all experiencing a boom in private education. Why is this happening? Because the state is failing to provide a decent education for children. For example, in rural Indian schools, a quarter of the teachers were reportedly absent. In Africa, teacher absenteeism hovers around 15-25 percent. Pakistan discovered a few years ago that 17 percent, or 8,000, of the state schools were actually non-existent. In Sierra Leone, one-fifth of the people on the state payroll are "ghost" teachers.

An article featured in a 2015 edition of *The Economist* reported the presence of 120 operating private schools in Mathare, which is a sizeable slum in Nairobi that half a million people call home. There are no paved streets nor sanitation. These schools cost about $1 a week to attend, and the children's parents are happy about the alternative option. Who isn't happy about this? Governments, NGOs, and teachers' unions, who believe that private education should be subject to heavy regulation and, in general, should be discouraged. So why do these private schools exist? Because there is lot of evidence that public schools are not up to par.

James Tooley, who was part of a team that conducted research on the phenomenon of private education in numerous poor countries, wrote a book on the matter. In *The Beautiful Tree*, he describes a staggering network of underground private schools for the poor, focusing on India, Nigeria, Ghana, Kenya, and China. According to Tooley, the government education officials in these countries are not even aware of private schools for the poor. In Makoko, a shantytown in Nigeria, his team found 32 private schools that were unrecognized by the government. They estimate that 70 percent of Makoko's schoolchildren attend these schools. In India, between little stores and workshops, Tooley's team found small private schools, identifiable by handwritten signs pointing to them, even on the edge of slums. In Gansu, China, the state had 26 official schools, even though these researchers located 586.

The totality of the studies conducted by Tooley's team in third world countries gives us a few key findings: private school children scored higher on standardized tests, had smaller class sizes and less teacher absenteeism, but they were inferior to government schools in just one aspect: the provision of quality playgrounds. Though we live in a wholly different set of circumstances in the United States, these private sector efforts in third-world countries give us tangible examples of what happens when people band together and decide that if the government won't do what it needs to do, they'll take matters into their own hands. That is responsibility in action!

What this phenomenon also dispels is the myth that "for-profit" is synonymous with "unethical." As many poor parents grapple with the realities of their financial circumstances, the love for their children drives them to send them to "for-profit" schools rather than "free" government schools in these third world countries. Of course, we are looking at different values of a dollar, and different costs of education, but the sentiment remains the same: parents want what is good for their children. The entity or person providing a service, which in this case is an education, is not necessarily unethical or greedy for putting a price tag on providing that service. In fact, profit and charitableness, or an appeal to humanity, can exist together. As Frederic Bastiat stated in *Economic Harmonies*, "the profit of the one is the profit of the other."

So how do we approach the matter of school choice in the United States? First of all, the word "vouchers" has been widely misunderstood and even derided. Perhaps the program could be called something else. Whatever the name, the chosen schools would simply be required to satisfy certain important minimum standards set forth by the appropriate governmental unit in order to qualify to teach our children.

As a product of the public school system myself, and having been raised by parents who strongly supported public education, I was concerned about Dr. Friedman's proposal of a voucher system. At that first meeting, I told him that I worried it would undermine the public education of our children. He responded by asking me two questions. The first question was: "If you were the parent of college-age students, to what country would you want to send them to receive the best education possible?" My response was that it was probably the United States. He agreed. The second question was: "If you were the parent of high school-age students, to what country would you want to send them to receive the best education possible?" My response was that I was not sure, but it was probably not the United States.

He agreed again. Then he said that the reason for this result was that we have a choice in where we spend our money with our colleges and universities, but we do not have the same choice in our high schools because the government makes those decisions for us. Therefore, we have competition and innovation in colleges, but we do not in our high schools. From that moment on, I have been a supporter of school choice, parental choice, scholarships, results-based budgeting, school empowerment, weighted student formula, or whatever name is used. The reason it works is that schools have incentives to perform well, or they will go out of business.

A similar question that explains the reason why Dr. Friedman's proposed programs work is the following: "Who is better able to decide how your child should be educated, you or the government?" I believe this is an easy question to answer. Thus we should take steps for decisions about the education of our children to be made as locally as possible. That means that parents, local schools and support groups like the PTAs should be able to say how and where the money for the education of students is spent. Of course, that also means that the federal government should have no say whatsoever in these matters. The Founders agreed with this. If you critically and carefully look at the U.S. Constitution, you'll notice that the word "education" is not mentioned anywhere. For similar reasons, the state's decision-making powers should also be severely curtailed because in the area of education, because the more it is locally controlled, the better the quality.

So if Dr. Friedman had his way, all families would be able to receive a voucher that allows for school choice. We're far from that on a national scale, but one state actually came close to realizing Friedman's vision. The Nevada Education Savings Account Program, which was enacted in 2015, allowed families with public school students to choose an alternative. State funds were to be deposited into a bank account, a special account that could only be used for educational costs at participating institutions that have been approved. However, this initiative was quickly met with two lawsuits, and in 2016, the Nevada Supreme Court struck down the funding mechanism of the program, though upholding the constitutionality of the program itself. Today, the initiative is dormant until new legislation is passed to create a funding mechanism.

The first school choice initiative in the state of Montana was launched in 2015 as a tax-credit scholarship program. Among many families benefiting from the program was Kendra Espinoza, a single mother holding two jobs so she could afford private-school tuition for her daughters, as a result of inadequate performances at their public school. Her youngest daughter struggled, and her eldest was bullied, leading Kendra to enroll them both as students at Stillwater Christian School, a private school where they flourished. Because of the tax-credit scholarship program, the burden of her daughters' tuition was lessened. At least it was lessened until the Montana Department of Revenue drew a distinction between parochial (religious) and secular schools, arguing that the tax-credit program was not constitutional as it indirectly provided aid to religious groups. But in Montana 69 percent of qualifying private schools have a religious affiliation, so all of a sudden the scope of choice was diminished substantially. So Ms. Espinoza challenged this, and the state trial court agreed with her. However, the Montana Supreme Court reversed this, arguing that the tax-credit scholarship program violated a state constitutional provision barring state aid to parochial schools and churches.

This conflicting constitutional provision was part of a wave of amendments across dozens of states in the late 19th century to ban government aid to religious institutions, often grouped and referred to as "Blaine Amendments." This referred to Senator James G. Blaine of Maine, who wanted to have a similar amendment added to the U.S. Constitution, but failed to do so. At the time, public schools followed a curriculum that sympathized with Protestantism, which were then known as "common schools." This affiliation wasn't cloaked either. Students were led into daily prayers by their teachers, religious hymns were sung, and the King James Bible was a point of reference. The religious institutions that Blaine Amendments targeted were primarily Catholic schools because, at the time, a strong anti-Catholic sentiment was an American reality. But what's staggering about this is the irony. School choice grew out of the initiatives of Catholic immigrants who wanted their children's education to espouse similar values, and now the outcome was reversed: exclusion from school choice programs was based upon a person's religious affiliation.

So does school choice violate the doctrine of the Separation of Church and State? Actually, no. This would be no different than Veterans choosing where their GI Bill benefits were to be spent, whether their colleges be UCLA, Notre Dame, Temple University, or Holy Cross. Why? Because it is the Veteran who is choosing, not the government. School Choice for K-12 is no different. For those uncertain if any rights are truly being curtailed here, consider the polar opposite: where the tax-credit scholarship program would only be applicable to religious private schools. That's the imposition or favoring of a religious group, a failure of separating church and state. A parent, however, should be allowed to choose regardless of the school's religious affiliation.

Fortunately, on June 30, 2020, the Supreme Court of the United States heard and decided the case. Espinoza v. Montana Department of Revenue was decided 5-4 in favor of Kendra, reversing and remanding the Montana Supreme Court ruling. This decision is a wonderful victory for school choice, and an excellent legal precedent for Liberty!

Today, there are 65 operational educational choice programs in 28 states, the District of Columbia, and Puerto Rico. In addition, there are almost an additional million families who are using individual tax credits and deductions for educational expenses that are achieving the same results. Milwaukee, for example, launched its Parental Choice Program in 1990, which is considered the first modern private school choice program in the nation. For three decades now, seventy-five percent of low-income families with children have enrolled and benefited from that Parental Choice Program. And this is just one of many programs that impact the lives of American families. So, once again, Liberty works, both from a philosophical standpoint as well as a practical one.

Under school choice, if your child is not interested in preparing for a university-trained career but would be successful with a career in the performing arts, you, as the parent, would have the choice to use your child's educational funds to pay for that type of schooling. The same would be true for other marketable skills like industrial arts, computer programming, mechanics, farming, nursing, and a wide variety of other vocations. As a practical matter, if there are enough students in a particular location who want to pursue a particular vocation, someone will customize a program to satisfy them, whether it be in person or online with interactive technology. As a result, parents will soon be able to choose the learning styles that match their children's abilities, interests, and motivations.

So why can't many government schools perform as well as schools that are forced to compete? Because, conceptually, government schools are funded from the top down. The government gives them money, which means there is no competition for that money. In that system, the administrators naturally have a tendency to funnel more of the money toward the administration. Then, in turn, the better teachers see this and naturally seek promotions into administrative positions for the higher pay. As a result, many of the better teachers are promoted out of the classrooms.

Of course, the implementation of a school choice policy is complicated and there will be problems that arise. For example, should all students be allocated the same amount of money for their education? No, probably special needs children would be allocated larger amounts, within reasonable limits. In addition, when students get older they usually require more funding for things like chemistry labs, foreign languages, and higher mathematics training, so each grade level might receive different funding. But all students in each grade level would receive the same allotment. Of course, that funding could also be augmented by the parents if they have the ability and choose to do so. So would the wealthy have access to better education? Yes, but that has been and always will be true. No system can change that reality.

Another problem area is that if schools must perform, they might be susceptible to "teaching for the test" in order to show parents that their children are achieving. In reality, we already have these same problems under our present system. So, what else is new?

The final perceived problem area is that many people fear that the parents of economically poor students will not care enough to find and use the better schools. That may be true for some but not for most. Actually, when different "gate" school opportunities have been available in the poorer economic areas, large numbers of those parents usually responded by camping out for a few days so they can obtain those special positions for their children. Finally, as a practical matter, if some parents who are not so motivated about their own children's education actually see that their neighbor's children are leaving a failing school for a different one, they'll probably follow along, if only because "I want to go where my friends go!"

We as a nation must decide what the purpose is for our educational system: educating our children or protecting below-average teachers. Tragically, we all know that for decades we have chosen the latter. But it should be a fundamental liberty for parents to have the choice of where and how the government money will be spent to educate their children. If they were to be so empowered, they would demand excellence and, if the results seen in 64 school choice programs around the country are to be believed, they would receive it! How does that happen? Ask yourself, how is it that today we have high quality computers, cell phones and automobiles on the market for a reasonable price? The answer is, of course, that we have competition in those industries. Education is no different.

Parents should be empowered to choose the best schools to meet the needs of their children, whether the schools be public, private, military, religious or vocational, as long as fundamental educational standards are met for teaching, "reading, writing, and arithmetic."

So who is against the idea of competition in our nation's schools? Well, in the first place it is against the "common wisdom." In my view, that will be counteracted simply by explaining to everyone the inherent advantages of the bottom-up as opposed to the top-down systems. Once people understand those benefits, they will change their views and demand school choice.

The only major remaining source of resistance to the idea will come from the present administrations and the teachers' unions that now control the government schools. It is not in their economic interest for that change to occur, particularly the unions, which selfishly continue to resist any reforms in favor of merit pay for more effective teachers, or to make it easier to terminate teachers who are not performing.

For the reasons outlined above, let's follow the lead of our Founders, as well as Milwaukee and other school districts. It is time for some real change. Once we pry the control of our schools away from the governmental and union bureaucrats, that control will be returned to parents and local agencies where it will be used more effectively and economically. If we do that, I am convinced that only good things will follow for all of our children throughout our country.

Chapter 8

Liberty and Our Children

We of the older generation are mostly doing pretty well financially. Many of our houses are paid for, we have investments, often good 401Ks or other retirement plans, and our Medicare and Social Security are paid for — mostly by younger workers. But the way things are financially today, Medicare and Social Security will simply not be available when younger workers are anywhere close to our ages. In addition, with the situation surrounding retirement pensions for federal, state, and local government workers, almost all of our governments literally will be bankrupt by the time our children are even close to middle age. But guess who will be forced to shoulder the burden of bailing our country out from this financial irresponsibility? Our children and grandchildren! What a legacy we are leaving them!

I have four children: William P. Gray (Bill), is named after my father and married to his wife Carla, Edward Ky Gray, who we adopted from Vietnam in 1973, Jennifer Marie Gray, though we call her Jenny, and Morgan M. Maeder and his wife Nikki, who recently welcomed a son, and thus my grandson, Hudson. And as I said several times on the Libertarian Presidential Debates, Hudson was born owing $73,000 due to the deficit, so I told him to "Pay Up!" And every day the amount we saddle our next generation with grows —

especially with these COVID-19 problems. The financial responsibility provided by Libertarians is the only hope in sight to protect the future solvency of our young people.

Additional problems are found by what many parents are doing too often today in "childproofing" the development of their own children. What does that mean? Because of fears that their children will be hurt or harmed, many parents don't allow them to walk to school by themselves, play unescorted in parks where they can make up games to play with their friends, go to a market or travel on public transportation unchaperoned, climb trees, or generally learn how to take care of themselves until dark when it's "time to come home for dinner," which was the rule when I was growing up.

Furthermore, during my childhood there were no terms like "Helicopter Parents," and my friends and I were not protected by "safe spaces" or from "trigger words" so that we could be kept from being confronted or otherwise forced to think on the spot for ourselves. Yes, we certainly want our children to be safe, but in too many ways many of us have overdone it. Not only do these "protections" breed a lack of ingenuity, creativity and independence, they also develop in many children a fear of life itself unless there is plenty of structure and supervision. So what good is Liberty if people are too fearful even after they have "grown up" to give it a try? Yes Liberty can be scary in lots of ways, but it still is the best and most productive and gratifying way to live our lives.

Of course, there are many things where I am not an expert, and parenting and mentoring children is certainly on that list. But taking from my experience both as a parent and as a judge on the Juvenile Court and with Peer Court, I have gathered some thoughts over the years as to what works in that regard. Naturally, the most critical element to the positive development of our children is loving them. But there are certainly some additional approaches I'd like to suggest.

First, we must teach our children the critical lesson that it's fun to learn. The more you learn, the more you see that everything in life is inter-connected. And that makes life much more fascinating and interesting. As an example, one of the countless things to marvel about is the human body, which is the most amazing machine in existence. There are reasons why our bodies do things for our protection without our conscious effort. With an education, we will get an exposure to questions like why do we cough? Well, if something is caught in our throats, a cough will help dislodge it. And our bodies vomit to get rid of poisons or things that are harming our stomachs. If you think about it, our bodies are fascinating, but we are much less likely to share in those wonders without an education.

Another critical guideline to teach our children is to "Eschew Mediocrity." I know this word is pompous, but I used it for emphasis in my high school musical "Americans All," and it worked. Make excellence a pattern so if people know that, for example, Ellen did a particular job, they would know that it had been done right. Thus, "Good Enough" seldom is good enough. One way to accomplish that outcome is to require all children to have regular chores to perform from an early age and be sure they are consistently done and done well. Once again, excellence is a learned pattern of conduct.

As stated above in our Peer Court discussion, ask teenagers to close their eyes and think about the three people they hang out with the most. And, without telling you who they are, ask the question: "Do you think they will be successful in their lives?" If not, maybe you should hang out with a different group of people. Another approach is to ask the question: "What is a friend?" Does someone who encourages you to shop lift a CD, be truant from school or lie about your conduct really a "friend?" Maybe that person is just a former friend, or maybe has always just been an acquaintance. These lines of questioning will help your children see that the people they surround themselves with will reflect upon themselves and affect their futures.

Children need boundaries, must know where those boundaries are, and how those boundaries will be enforced. But then most children will flourish within those boundaries! In addition, teenagers expect their parents to parent and are inwardly disappointed when they don't. Some parents are amazed at this thought, as they have instead simply tried to be their children's "friends." But that is not at all the same thing!

Ask teenagers how old they are right now, and then how old they will be ten years from now. Then ask them what they want their lives to look like ten years from now. We all know that those ten years will go by quickly, but for a teenager it will seem like an eternity. So, if you want to be an engineer, attorney, mechanic or medical doctor, what are you doing right now to further those worthwhile goals? And will shoplifting at Target help you achieve them? The sooner adolescents realize that dreams don't work unless they do, the more time they'll have to find opportunities that lead them to their goals.

In addition, children should be taught and shown that it often pays to postpone gratification. People who can do that are much more likely to be successful than those who cannot. And when things go poorly along the way, teach children not to cry or whine, but to express themselves using words. And when they do fall down, teach them how to get up on their own without fawning over them (unless they are truly hurt). Of course, grandparents should strongly to assist in the development of children, but it is also their entitlement, if not their firm obligation, to spoil the grandchildren. So do it without apology!

The best thing a father can do for his children is to love their mother. When looking for a mate, project who you would like to be the mother/father of your children. That approach alone has changed numbers of lives — for the better. The classic father is gentle beneath his firmness, and the classic mother is firm beneath her gentleness.

In addition, although it may for some people not be politically correct to discuss this issue so bluntly, one of the best things that parents can do for their children is to be married to each other. How and with whom people live if they are not parents I leave to their own sense of morals and views of Liberty. But if people have children, they owe it to their children to be legally as well as morally committed to each other in marriage. I am aware that marriage and family life are considered private issues. But they are also a part of the public arena because of the negative outcomes that are associated with non-marital births, the primary one being a lack of financial stability, which public policy has sought to ameliorate since the 1960s.

Without the commitment of marriage, in so many ways the children of those parents are virtually condemned to having lives of substantially-reduced opportunities. That is without even considering the many women who wind up taking care of children without a supportive partner. And, tragically, today's social mores appear almost routinely to accept this as the status quo. The most recent CDC data found that 39.6% of all births in the United Stated are to unwed mothers. Of those births, 28.2% of mothers are Caucasian, 51% are Hispanic, and 69.4% are African-Americans. Research has shown that single parent families have lower median incomes, and that their children suffer both academically and behaviorally.

So what can we do about this? We should hammer this thought into the children we can influence from an early age, and when we hear laudatory reports about male celebrities who have children "with their girlfriends," we should respond with sadness and even shame. This issue should not be left to religious and spiritual leaders alone, each of us must all vocally do our part. Liberty comes with responsibilities, and where better to place our efforts than the future of so many of our children?

One of the most important choices a young person must make is whether to continue or drop out of school. It is a fact of life that the dropout rates of our young people from high schools, even in some upper-level economic areas, are bafflingly high, and that is an area of legitimate concern. In many discussions I've had with junior high and high school-age children I tell them that right at this moment each one of them has a job. What is it, I ask? They mostly stumble and stammer in their responses, but with time they come up with what I view to be the correct answer: their job is to get an education. It is probably the most important job they will ever have.

Remind those who are not concentrating on their studies that millions of young people their age all around the world would give up anything for the opportunities that they seem to be throwing away. There are so many people rooting for our children, including their parents, family, friends, and people they do not know — like me. I want them to get a good education. So do you.

And yes, there are more people who are rooting for them as well. Talking with a boy, I say that there's a girl out there who may not even know you yet, but she is genuinely hoping that you get a good education. Why? Because it will make an extremely important difference in her life. Who might that be? Of course, his future wife or significant other is the answer, and for the boy it is the same thing as to their future wife or significant other. And that is not even talking about their future children.

It's no secret that education level and future earnings go hand in hand. On average, people who graduate only from elementary school earn about $595,700 during their entire lifetimes. But if those people stay in school and get just a high school degree, that number nearly doubles. Then if they go on to college, on the average they will make much more than double that amount again to about $2,846,300. Thus, dropping out of school is a choice, and that choice will have a big effect upon these young people and their eventual families for the rest of their lives. Confront them: would you like to have a better-paying job and more interesting life? Stay in school. Education is your key.

Outside of the classroom, the two best ways to expand our children's horizons are traveling and reading. In traveling they are exposed to unfamiliar places and see both the bad and the good of how other people live. That allows them to learn firsthand that there are places in the world other than where they were raised, and both be stimulated by the differences and more appreciative of what they have here at home. In reading they can vicariously live the lives of other beings of any time and any place, and this will bring them a much deeper understanding of their own lives and the world around them. And, besides, reading really is fun!

When I was 12 years old, my parents took my older sister and me to Europe for six weeks. We took the train from Los Angeles to New York, and then a passenger ship to England. Our parents did it this way so that my sister and I could see firsthand how large our country is, and how far away Europe is from us. Then we traveled in England, Scotland, France, Switzerland (the birthplace of my mother's grandparents) and Denmark before flying home.

That trip more than anything else in my life filled me with both a wanderlust and the knowledge that, as time went on, I could travel by myself too. It was a great thing for my development and my independence. What a lasting gift my parents gave us by this trip!

A question I frequently ask other people is, "Where is the most fascinating place you have ever been?" Then I say they can define fascinating any way they want to. The responses to that questions have almost always been interesting. In fact, I asked that question to Dr. Eugen Weber, who was my favorite UCLA professor, and his wife. They both responded that their most fascinating place was the Villa d'Este on Lake Como in Northern Italy. Several years later my wife and I went there expressly because of their answer. And the Webers were right. Other than being quite expensive, it was a truly wonderful and stimulating place.

My most fascinating place is Aphrodisias, which is in the Asian side of Turkey. This was an eighth century B.C. Greek city named for Aphrodite, who was the Greek goddess of love. It absolutely captured me with its stadium, theater, forum, temples, baths, and stories. Trying to project what life was actually like in this fascinating place continues to fill me with inspiration and wonder.

What are your favorite books for children? If we do not help instill in our children a love of reading at a fairly young age, they will be deprived of one of life's most fascinating and rewarding pleasures (and parenthetically their scores on the SAT and similar tests will truly suffer).

By the way, don't forget to join a book discussion club of about five to seven people. I recommend you have dinner together once a month, and then gather around and discuss a book that has been assigned and read by everyone for that session. There is virtually no limit to the enjoyment and stimulation you will experience, as well as bonding.

So do a big favor for your children, grandchildren and other people you care about, and expose them to books. The best way to do that is to read to and with them and at an early age. When I was on the Abused and Neglected Children's Calendar in Juvenile Court, I purchased numbers of copies of the book Fox in Socks by Dr. Seuss, and gave them to the children's parents, grandparents, or foster parents with strict instructions to read the book to and with them while the children were sitting on their laps. This is a wonderful, fun, and silly tongue-twister of a book that lends itself perfectly to group reading. I think it worked, and I strongly recommend this book and this practice be used by all guardians of children.

What are other books that are great for children? My favorites are Jack London's *White Fang*, Pearl Buck's *The Good Earth*, both Mark Twain's *Tom Sawyer* and *Huckleberry Finn*, Frank Baum's *The Wizard of Oz* (Our wonderful father read the entire series of these books to us as children.) and Wilson Rawls' *Where the Red Fern Grows*. Many people also recommend C.S. Lewis' *The Lion, the Witch, and the Wardrobe* and Dave Pelzer's *A Child Called 'It'*, although I think the latter book is pretty depressing for a young child.

Although reading is one of the most fun and bonding things a person can do with young children, I acknowledge traveling with them is not always that much fun, at least at the beginning. But once you start seeing the expansion of their development and general interest in life, you will fully know you have given them a great and lasting gift. So help to expand the horizons of the children in your life. It is one of the best gifts that a person can give, or that a child can receive.

But there's another growing problem area for many children in the United States that I feel compelled to address: the obesity crisis. Seventeen percent of U.S. children are obese, a staggering figure, though they aren't short of company given that 42.4% of U.S. adults are obese. Childhood obesity often isn't just a stand-alone condition either. It increases the child's likelihood of developing high blood pressure, high cholesterol, type 2 diabetes, breathing problems, joint problems, and psychological distress. The reason for the persistence of this issue is that many of our children are less physically active, subjected to more stress, and eat more harmful foods and fewer fruits and vegetables. Recent data from the Centers for Disease Control and Prevention has indicated that, for the first time in U.S. history, children will have a shorter life expectancy than their parents. Though smoking is the leading preventable cause of death and disease in our country, obesity comes in a close and competitive second.

Fortunately, obesity can also be preventable and there are some easy and straightforward remedies to this epidemic. Those remedies are well-known to us all: better nutrition and more daily exercise. But it's not really up to our children to figure that out. The onus is on the adults! Parents must take the initiative for change in their own households.

Not only private lives are deeply affected by this issue, the economy is too. In 2018 alone, $480.7 billion was spent in direct health-care costs for the management of obesity or obesity-caused conditions. If that number was shocking to you, consider the estimated $1.24 trillion that is lost in productivity. This isn't a new problem. To the contrary, obesity has been a topic of conversation for about two decades. Aside from a brief pause between 2009 and 2012, obesity rates in our country to climb.

Given the high costs of this condition, where does government fit in? There have been urgent calls for a federal policy to keep our waistlines in check. Some even propose a 'fat tax' on unhealthy foods and sodas. Others urge the display of caloric and nutritional information in restaurants and other points of food and beverage sale (which I actually favor). But I, and my fellow Libertarians, will point out that federal regulation and food policy already exists, and it has done nothing to stop us from getting fat.

But some other countries, however, have taken unique policy approaches to reducing obesity as a public health issue. For example, in 2008, Japan's national data indicated an upward trend in weight. So the Japanese government appealed to paternalism, passing the "Metabo Law," which requires overweight people or those with weight-related illnesses to attend dieting classes. If they do not show up for the classes, their employers and/or local government must pay fines to the federal government. Additionally, companies surpassing a certain percentage of overweight workers are fined by the government. While such a policy would likely not be welcomed with open arms in our country, it's a punitive incentive to Japanese employers, workers, local governance, and individuals to keep their waistlines in check. The United Arab Emirates launched a weight-loss incentive campaign in 2013 titled "Your Weight in Gold." Targeting adults and children alike, this national Biggest Loser contest rewarded each kilogram lost with a gram of gold. The campaign ended in 2015, and to date is the most expensive public health campaign in the region, awarding around $2.5 million in gold to successful participants.

But I don't think it is hard to imagine that a policy like Japan's would fly here, and I certainly hope not! As I mentioned, the practical solution is personal responsibility in the form of diet and exercise, as well as our governments providing us with timely and accurate information. Since we all know this now, why haven't Americans lost more weight? At its most fundamental, many of us have chosen poorly. New Year's Resolutions anybody?

My parents, Elizabeth and Bill Gray

With my parents in the summer of 1957

As a Lieutenant in the JAG Corps, U.S. Naval Reserve

My return to Palmar Norte, Costa Rica
where I had served in the Peace Corps

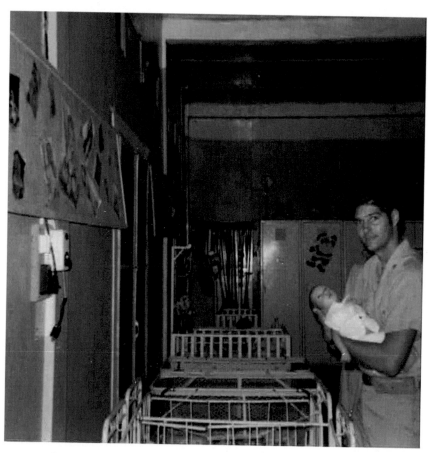

With my son Ky at the orphanage in Danang, Vietnam in 1972

My children, Ky, Jenny, and Bill

This Time, It's a Labor of Love for the Judge

By KENNETH FREED
Times Staff Writer

On most occasions, swearing in new citizens is part of the job of being a federal judge, a nice part, but still something that comes with the black robe.

But Friday, the job became pure pleasure for U.S. Dist. Judge William P. Gray. For among the 1,063 people he swore in as new Americans was a 7-year-old boy, Edward Ky Gray, the judge's grandson.

Ky, as he is called, was an orphaned Vietnamese baby in 1973 when Gray's son James adopted him. Now, Gray said Friday, "it is my cherished privilege to participate" in the oath-taking ceremony making Ky a citizen.

With the new Americans nearly filling the orchestra section of the plush and opulent Dorothy Chandler Pavilion, Gray sat at a table on the stage. Ky and his brother and sister, Billy and Jenny, sat next to him.

When it came time to take the oath, Ky stood up and raised his right hand. But the words—talk about obligations and abjuring former sovereigns—seemed too much and his lips hardly moved.

But at the end, the judge gave him a hearty handshake and so did brother Billy.

Gray, who with his chiseled features and full gray hair, is the very model of a judicial magistrate, talked about citizenship.

"It means for you a fulfillment of a dream," he said, and "a great day for our country."

Unlike those people who were born in the United States and had no choice but to be Americans, Gray explained, "you have sought to become citizens because you were attracted to the principles of freedom and justice."

Gray then discussed the duties as well as privileges of citizenship in remarks perhaps symbolizing our times.

"Be careful for whom you vote," he said, "pay your taxes and conserve fuel."

GRANDSON BECOMES AN AMERICAN—U.S. Dist. Judge William Gray holds Edward Ky Gray, 7, after swearing in the boy and 1,0 other persons as new citizens in Dorothy Chandler Pavilion. Edwa was a Vietnam orphan when judge's son, James, adopted hi
STORY IN PART II, PAGE 1   Times photo by Jayne Ke

My son Ky becomes an American citizen in 1979

My father, Judge William A. Gray,
swearing me in as a Judge in January, 1984

Fly fishing

BUSINESS LITIGATION SECTION

1992 JUDGE OF THE YEAR

JAMES P. GRAY

WAS HONORED DECEMBER 4, 1992 AT THE BUSINESS LITIGATION SECTION MEETING. THIS SECTION MEETS THE 1ST FRIDAY OF EVERY MONTH. FOR INFORMATION CALL 541-6222.

▲ THE HONORABLE JAMES P. GRAY ACCEPTS THE CONGRATULATIONS OF BUSINESS LITIGATION SECTION CHAIR, PAT O'KEEFE

TIM CAPPEL INTRODUCES JUDGE TED MILLARD'S COMMENTS ON "ABUSIVE LAWYERS." ▼

THE PANEL CONSISTING OF (L-R) TIM CAPPEL, JUDGE TED MILLARD, JUSTICE THOMAS CROSBY AND ROBERT COLDREN DISCUSS "FRIVOLOUS LAWSUITS." ▶

▼ INCOMING CHAIR, GEORGE PIGGOT PRESENTS PAT O'KEEFE A PLAQUE FOR HIS DEDICATION & SERVICE TO THE BUSINESS LITIGATION SECTION.

▲ 1993 CHAIR-ELECT ROBERT E. PALMER EXPRESSES HIS APPRECIATION.

PHOTOS BY RANDALL CHOCO & LORI SHEPLER

1992 Judge of the Year

Speaking at the Hoover Institution on Drug Policy in 1993

Rally during my 1998 Congressional campaign

With my wife Grace at our wedding

With my wife Grace and our son Morgan
in New Zealand, 2002

Jim's plans for returning our nation to peace, prosperity and freedom are documented in his book,

A Voter's Handbook: Effective Solutions to America's Problems
The Forum Press, 2010

Judge James P. Gray (Ret.)

Both parties have beaten Old Glory **red, black** and **blue.**

Citizens of all stripes are poised to **strike a blow for liberty.**

I stand with you – **ready and able.**

Every President represented on Mt. Rushmore was elected from outside the reigning political establishment of the day.

Thomas Jefferson knew his **stuff.**

Since you're a participant in this event today, you require no fresh reminders of how rapidly those in control of Washington are erasing the last remnants of the Constitutional protections this nation was founded upon.

America is now living the threat Thomas Jefferson repeatedly warned us about. The man authored the U.S. Constitution. It's time to take his advice on how best to restore it.

During the revolutionary war, 12% of the colonists did the fighting while the other 88% sat back and watched. **It's up to US to rally the sleeping majority.**

Revolution 2
Liberty needs all of US

Judge of the Year. Peace Corps Volunteer. Author. Ready.

Libertarian

Jim GRAY
VICE PRESIDENT

Find out more about Judge Jim Gray at: www.JudgeJimGray.com

Flyer from my campaign for Vice-President
alongside Gary Johnson in 2012

Speaking at the World Affairs Council of Orange County

Chapter 9

Liberty and War

War is not glorious. And with war, of course, comes coldly arbitrary destruction and deaths and serious injuries which, in turn, exact a lasting cost not only for combatants who sustain both visible and non-visible wounds, but also to many of the people whom the combatants come back to or leave behind. Thus war is devoutly to be avoided, if at all possible. Nevertheless, and even with those understandings firmly in mind, there are some values that must constantly be fought for. And foremost among those are our national safety and protecting our national interests which, vitally, include Liberty. But tragically, and realistically, there are and have always been people in power who see a reluctance in others to go to war as a sign of weakness. And almost never can those people be appeased. Sometimes the threat of war or even war itself is necessary. But it is the sacred obligation of our national leaders to only pursue war when our core national issues are truly involved.

Is our country at war? That is a question that must be asked, because there are many important consequences for being at war. So are we? Well, the answer is no, we are not at war and have not been since World War II. The explanation for that answer is actually quite simple and straightforward: Congress has not issued a Declaration of War since December 1941. Article I, Section 8 of the United States

Constitution expressly mandates that only Congress can issue such a declaration, and it has indisputably not done so since 1941. Passing various war powers resolutions is not the same thing as a declaration. So in the first place, our country was not at war in Vietnam or Iraq and is not now at war in Afghanistan and, secondly, since one simply cannot effectively be at "war" against a thing, an idea, or a loosely knit group of people that is not a nation, we are also not involved in a so-called "War on Terrorism", "War on Drugs," or "War on Coronavirus" either.

Mr. Larry Sharpe, a fellow member of the Libertarian Party and a friend, was a guest on my podcast on June 26, 2020. One of many things we spoke about was fear, and he said: "What the American people want is safety. Why? We are afraid. We are afraid of China, afraid of COVID, afraid of one another. We want safety." Such a concept is a great thing for politicians to rally against, but otherwise it serves no practical or positive purpose except to scare people and to concentrate more power in the hands of the politicians. And, of course, to serve as a vehicle to get politicians elected and re-elected.

Some people have argued that this is a naïve approach to today's life and that, as a practical matter, Congress has declared war by delegating its war-making decisions to the president. So, they argue, the declaration requirement in the Constitution is just an unnecessary formality. While it is true that there were no declarations of war before we fought in Korea, Vietnam, Panama, Serbia, the Persian Gulf, or anywhere else since 1941, this is not an unimportant distinction. The drafters of the Constitution not only were not naïve, they were brilliant. They knew that the decision about whether to go to war or not is one of the most critical decisions that can be made. That is why they required the protections of a specific procedure to be followed before that event could occur.

Of course, every war will always have its dissenters, and that certainly included World War II. But regardless of where each person may stand on the issue of our military intervention in Iraq, had we followed the mandates of the Constitution and placed the issue of whether or not actually to declare war upon the regime of Saddam Hussein directly before Congress, our country and the world would clearly be in a better position today. And that would be true, no matter what Congress' decision had been.

A request to Congress from the President for a Declaration of War would certainly have been followed by a fuller debate than the ones we had both in Congress and around the country. Questions would have been asked, and reasons and alternatives explored. For example, is the regime of Saddam Hussein a serious threat to the security and wellbeing of the United States? If so, is actual war the best way to combat that threat, or are there other viable alternatives? If we go to war, what are our goals, and how will we know when those goals have been achieved? Once we have succeeded militarily, what should we do to keep the peace? What are the important areas to protect right after the fall of the Hussein regime, such as ammunition depots, museum artifacts, electric power generating facilities, etc. Also, is it more important as well as less costly to put the people of Iraq back to work building and rebuilding their country themselves, instead of awarding those contracts to large American companies?

Another clear benefit had we followed the dictates of the Constitution would be that the people of our country would quite likely have been much more united behind the effort had Congress decided to declare war after a full debate. That would almost certainly have been true for Vietnam as well. This reality cannot be understated. Now it is certainly true that Congress has passed some resolutions since World War II allowing military force to be used in different places at the discretion of the president. One of the most famous was the Gulf of Tonkin Resolution that allowed President Lyndon Johnson directly to commit troops to fight in Vietnam without a Declaration of War. Others were when Congress affirmed the 1991 War Resolution passed by the United Nations and thereby allowed the first President Bush to commit troops in the liberation of Kuwait; the Iraq Liberation Act of 1998 under President Clinton that stated it was the policy of the United States to seek a regime change in Iraq and to promote a democratic government in its place; and the Iraq Resolution in 2002 that allowed the second President Bush to send military troops to fight in Iraq. And it is also true that these were preceded by some debates.

But we cannot and must not go to war on the sly. Passing resolutions does not take nearly the courage that passing a Declaration of War does. In fact, today a post office bill seems to get more congressional deliberation than passing a resolution to send American troops into armed conflict. And, make no mistake about it, this situation is not the fault of a president. The pressure on our nation's presidents to keep us safe is overwhelming. No, it is the members of Congress that have failed in their constitutional duty.

Basically, Congress wants to have the power without the responsibility for their actions. Shame on them all! Were our "military police actions" in places like Vietnam, Korea, Panama, Iraq, and Afghanistan really necessary to protect our National Security or National Interests? In that regard, I firmly believe that at least our invasion of Iraq (which was the biggest foreign policy mistake in my lifetime) would not have passed that test. Probably not Vietnam either. And, although Congress probably would have passed one after the attack on September 11, 2001, it almost certainly would have limited our troops to going into Afghanistan, finding Osama bin Laden and his cohorts, annihilating them, and then withdrawing from that country — along with the warning that we would return and do so again if they remained a threat.

So, why does the distinction of whether or not the President should file a Congressional request for a declaration of war even matter? Once again, the drafters of our Constitution were brilliant. Today many people, even citizens of our country, are being imprisoned for indefinite periods of time without charges being filed against them and without them having access to attorneys or our courts. We have also seen the interception of telephone calls of our citizens from here to other countries, and we have all heard allegations of kidnappings and torture at the hands of some agents of our government. And all of these actions have been justified because "we are at war."

In August 2018, the *New York Times* published an opinion piece by Matt Welch, an editor of *Reason Magazine*, about the teachings of the late Senator John McCain on the subject of torture. He said that McCain taught us that torture, "produces faulty intelligence," that "every man has a breaking point," and that military personnel derive a motivational pride from America having higher moral standards than its debased adversaries. "Your last resistance, the one that sticks, the one that makes the victim superior to the torturer, is the belief that were the positions reversed you wouldn't treat them as they have treated you." We must continue to learn from McCain, because interest in this important issue appears to have waned. And it should not because, as McCain said, "This is a moral debate. It is about who we are."

The prison at Guantanamo is still open, much to our discredit! Contrary to our values, it was opened under President George W. Bush, maintained by President Obama, and President Trump signed an executive order in 2018 to keep it open. So do we care? Have we learned from Senator McCain that unaccountable power behaves unaccountably? Yes, we know that after Osama bin Laden was located and killed, many officials in our government widely spouted that this never would have happened without using "Enhanced Interrogation Techniques." But was this true? Ask McCain, who subsequently wrote: "In truth, most of the C.I.A.'s claims that abusive interrogations of detainees had produced vital leads to help locate Bin Laden were exaggerated, misleading, and in some case, complete bullshit." But even if it worked, the very soul of the United States of America is its Freedoms and its Liberties. Do we not believe that our soul is under direct attack if we do not treat everyone in our custody humanely? Of course, we should also define what we mean by the word torture because there is a significant difference between breaking bones, on the one hand, and subjecting people to sleep deprivation and loud music on the other. But in the end, it is not about other people, other countries, or even the Geneva Convention, it's about who we are! And I believe we are better than this! What do you think?

Of course, some of the people in our custody are dangerous. But our response should take into consideration a saying we used back in the days that I was a federal prosecutor "If you lie down in the gutter with dogs, you'll get up with fleas." If we lower ourselves to the level of those radical people who would do us ill, we will get up in the morning with the same fleas that have infested them. In addition, Osama bin Laden would be pleased because, by pursuing these actions, we are actually accomplishing some of his goals for him. How so? Because we are showing the world that we are no better than most other countries. The soul of the United States of America is in our freedoms and constitutional protections, and if we do not uphold these safeguards to liberty, we will no longer be a beacon for a better world.

Is there a threat by Al-Qaeda, ISIS, and other similar organizations to our country and to our safety and well-being? Undeniably, the answer is yes. But as a fact of life, we simply cannot protect ourselves from every threat that the zealots and cowards of this world might be able to concoct. Yes, we can attempt to control bombings on our commercial airliners and we should try to do so. But what about in every train station? Does anyone really think that even if we give up all of our constitutional protections that we can possibly protect every highway bridge or tunnel in our country from a terrorist act, or every theater, stadium, school or shopping mall? The Soviet Union tried to do this in Afghanistan and Chechnya and failed, and so would we.

The answer is to treat these threats and even attacks as the critically important police matters that they are. The primary protection against them is good intelligence, and we have been derelict in reducing the capabilities of our nation's intelligence-gathering community. Additional protections come from all of us being vigilant, and training and equipping our law enforcement officers in the best manner possible. But otherwise, we must be mature and sophisticated in understanding that there are some threats in life from which there are no protections, and we should then go on about our normal lives.

Furthermore, saying this is a matter for the police does not at all mean that we are minimizing the potential threats. Even though criminal gangs like those of Al Capone, the Crips, and the Bloods have presented definite and even severe threats to public safety, Congress did not declare war against them. It is a police matter. The same is true for groups of people like ISIS that are basically non-nation states. Of course, if Al-Qaeda had the protection of the government of a country like Afghanistan on September 11, 2001, when it committed an act of war upon the people of our country on our soil, in my opinion we had every right to respond as we did. But Congress should first have declared war before we did so.

In addition, just because these are matters for the police does not mean they will only be handled by the local sheriff. The FBI and CIA are police and law enforcement agencies, and they certainly will all be called upon to enforce our nation's laws and hold people accountable for their actions. So the matters will still be taken seriously, but without all of the push for reducing our liberties because "We are at War!"

We must not give in to politics. We must understand that if politicians really wanted to reduce the ability of those radical people to harm us, they would do a major thing that would most cripple them: repeal Drug Prohibition. The primary funding for terrorists all around the world is the money received from the sale of illegal drugs. In fact, Drug Prohibition is literally the "Golden Goose" of terrorism. There will always be radical people in the world who want for whatever reason to harm us and others, but they will be a great deal less dangerous if we take away their funding. But politicians mostly still refuse even to discuss that fact of life.

Thus, again to repeat, we must follow the procedures brilliantly and forthrightly set forth by our Founders, which is to demand full disclosure, full debate and then a vote from Congress before we go to war. Then we will be justly committed as a country to the result, and God help those who stand in our way. So no, for the reasons discussed above we are not at war. But without a constitutional Declaration of War, we will also never be at peace, because these undeclared conflicts will politically never be allowed to end.

But what happens to those who risk their lives for our country, members of the Armed Forces? It's no secret that one of our national embarrassments is the way we have ignored the needs of our veterans over the years, particularly those who are mentally disabled or harmed. Today, when they are first wounded, the medical attention our troops receive from the military community is generally wonderful enough to bring tears to your eyes. But once the troops are stabilized and eventually discharged, the Veteran's Administration is simply not funded well enough to handle their remaining needs. Many of our troops returning from Iraq and Afghanistan come back with symptoms of brain injuries or post-traumatic stress disorder (PTSD), or what used to be called "shell shock." These problems are encountered in numerous ways, but one of the most prevalent is the concussions that come from being close to explosions. In fairness, for the most part the active duty military is taking this situation seriously, and is diagnosing and treating its troops as well as humanly possible. But once the troops have been discharged, the Veterans Administration has not had the resources to continue with this treatment.

As John A. Parrish, M.D. states in his book *Autopsy of War*, during the Vietnam era, traumatic brain injuries and even serious psychiatric disabilities were seldom even diagnosed, much less treated. But appreciable progress has been made since that time. And those improvements should make us all proud. Nevertheless, that progress in treatment for our active-duty personnel has not benefited many of our Veterans, and this is an egregious breach of contract.

What does the evidence show? Veterans are twice as likely to become homeless than other Americans. California, in particular, has a disproportionately large number of homeless veterans, making up approximately 35 percent of the homeless population in Orange and Los Angeles Counties. Furthermore, there is an average of 8,030 suicides per year (or 22 per day) of people who have left military service, and 69 percent of those are 50 years of age or older. And with more of our military personnel returning, those problems have seriously escalated, to the degree that a full one-quarter of our troops returning from those areas have at least one psychiatric disorder.

We are all aware of too many tragic examples of some of our military personnel going on a rampage. To paraphrase a former Marine who had returned home from Afghanistan after his unit had lost 14 of its troops in nine days, whose story I read in a newspaper years ago: "At first it's fear — fear of everything. Then you just go numb. Then you feel guilt. And then you start drinking and that causes even more trouble. I felt like the war made me into a monster, but I'm really not a monster." These returning troops need our help, and if that help does not come, the problems will often never go away.

So what must be done? First of all, if you were in military service and feel that you fit into this category, do not be embarrassed — or bashful. Call the V.A. Crisis Line at 800-273-8255 (TALK) and seek assistance! This includes all Vets who have headaches or anxiety, are unusually scared, or simply do not feel normal since their military service. In fact, if someone you know fits that description, help them to make that call.

Second, instead of making veterans show that their brain injuries or PTSD were incurred during their time of military service, require the government to show that they were not. Many Vietnam vets who had incurred disabilities were excluded from treatment, and many of those are the ones who have become homeless or suicidal. And the same thing has happened with other "wounded warriors" thereafter.

Third, the diagnosis, treatment and follow-up for brain injuries and PTSD take time and are expensive. So even though the federal government spends far too much money in far too many other areas, this is one area in which it must spend more.

These disabled men and women signed contracts to be in our military service and have answered our nation's call to protect our security and freedom. Our obligations, both legal and moral, are to take care of them if they have disabilities as a part of that military service — regardless of when that service was.

Fortunately, we are seeing some progress. The U.S. Department of Veterans Affairs has projected a 220-billion-dollar budget for the fiscal year 2020, a 9.6% increase from the year before. Recent numbers from the Department of Housing and Urban Development show that the number of homeless veterans has decreased two percent in the last year, and fifty percent since 2010. That's an improvement, and I hope that these efforts continue and expand.

Veterans aren't just important to Americans, Canadians also honor their patriots with a yearly tradition. I've come to know of it because of my great wife who was raised in Canada. She tells me that every November 11 since 1921 there has been a national celebration of Armistice Day or, as it is also known, either "Remembrance Day" or "Poppy Day." Thus, starting on about November 1, people all around the country and from every walk of life wear artificial red poppies on their clothing. This had its roots in the poem "In Flanders Fields" by a Canadian named Lieutenant Colonel John McCrae and which begins, "In Flanders Fields the poppies blow, between the crosses, row on row..." Thereafter, the tradition spread to much of the British Commonwealth. It is in remembrance of troops who have died, especially in World Wars I and II, but also in other military conflicts.

The red poppies are worn over the heart, with the red representing the blood of all those who gave their lives, the black representing the mourning for those who didn't return home, and the green leaf representing the grass and crops growing and future prosperity after the war had destroyed so much. The poppy is meant to be positioned at 11 o'clock to represent the eleventh hour of the eleventh day of the eleventh month. So, I suggest that we adopt that custom in our country as well! Let's unify and celebrate our troops who gave their ultimate contribution by universally thanking them at that time of year, nationwide! We should all agree that our fallen troops deserve forever to be honored, and this is how we can do it. And we can become more unified as a country along the way.

The three most patriotic places I have ever been in my life are the Arlington National Cemetery, Ellis Island, and the U.S.S. Arizona Memorial in Hawaii. Frankly, I got tears in my eyes and extra strength in my heart from my visits to each place. Especially at the U.S.S. Arizona, which has a memorial that is constructed lower in the

middle over the sunken battleship. This symbolizes the lowest ebb of
our morale and spirit when the ship went down, and higher on the
sides as we moved away from the tragedy. But as we honor those who
fought and continue to fight for our way of life, we must not let
patriotism drive us to impose our way on life on others. It would help
us to understand that realities have changed. We meddle too much,
and to our own detriment. I was the chair of the World Affairs Council
of Orange County, and prior to one of our meetings, I was talking to
the Consul General of both Germany and India. I asked them frankly,
"What do you think of the U.S?" The German Consul General
responded diplomatically, "We are partners and friends." I
responded by asking him what he really thought. The answer was far
more honest: "Your government mostly treats us like children, and is
always trying to tell us what to do." And the consul general of India
agreed. And they have a point. We are often quite nosy and not shy
about it.

Congressman Ron Paul said that the U.S. today has about 400
military reservations around the world. Yes, 400! Why? What are we
doing in all of these places? Let's audit them, publicly, and look at
them individually. If they are necessary fine, keep them or even
reinforce them. But, at this point, most of them probably are not.
Probably after just a 45-day audit we could determine that 300 of them
are simply not necessary such that they should be closed as long as
we wouldn't be breaking our agreements with the foreign countries.
If we would be, we could renegotiate, or we could leave after the
leases or agreements have expired. Those are things we need to do.

Take this as an example: I love New Zealand and I love New
Zealanders. But if New Zealand had a naval air station ten miles away
from my home, pretty soon I'd get tired of their jets noisily flying over

our house, or possibly inebriated sailors who might end up picking on our women. So soon, it's safe to say, I would probably stop liking New Zealanders quite so much. Other than the foreigners liking the money we spend in their countries, most of them feel the same way. Plus, most of the time we would actually be safer by bringing our troops home. In today's world we neither can nor should we try to police the world virtually by ourselves. This is true both because we can no longer afford it, and because we simply cannot impose our will upon others without their desire and cooperation.

Thus, our military policy should be controlled by two prongs. First, we should get involved militarily in various problem areas around the world only if the world community decides to participate in that action, unless that matter expressly affects our own national interests. Extremists like the Taliban are as much a threat to Germany, China, Russia, Turkey, and Japan as they are to us, and unless those countries choose to participate in whatever action is going to be taken, we should not be involved. Second, in places like Syria, Iraq, Iran, the Sudan, and others where extremists are attempting to impose their own selfish will, we should as publicly as possible let the people in those countries know that they will have to control their own destiny. Thus they can choose either to live with anarchy or with freedom, and act accordingly. We cannot, and do not want to, control their country, religious beliefs, or lives. We can join the world community in helping them to live in freedom, if they request it, but the fundamental choices about how they will live their lives will have to be made by them.

The end of a war marks a new point in time, one of potential change, for better or worse. I was briefly in Vietnam during the war, and in 2010 my wife Grace and I returned to Vietnam for a two-week trip. I was astounded by the extraordinary change that I observed. The first thing we noticed about Ho Chi Minh City (formerly Saigon) is the chaotic traffic: mostly motorbikes and motor scooters, but also lots of cars, trucks, and bicycles mixed in, and precious few traffic signals. So with these pesky two-wheelers darting all over the place, it's kind of like driving in spaghetti. But, amazingly enough, although we saw and experienced many near misses, we didn't see even one collision while we were there. And we didn't even see many scratches on the cars. So I guess their system is working.

We also saw that most of the Vietnamese women driving motor scooters wore a mask over their faces, long sleeves and gloves. The reason we were given was that having the fairest skin possible is considered to be much better looking in Vietnam. We also were told about an example of the true new Vietnamese (and American) entrepreneurial spirit. A few years ago, during the bird flu epidemic, the people in Vietnam simply stopped eating chicken. Many Kentucky Fried Chicken outlets compensated for that reality by importing their chickens from France, and publicizing that fact to encourage sales. But it didn't help. So until the epidemic waned, KFC became KFF, which stood for Kentucky Fried Fish. And they got along nicely.

The most sobering experience on our trip to Vietnam was a visit to the Cu Chi Tunnels, which were dug by the Viet Cong during the French occupation, and continued during the fighting with our troops. The Viet Cong were South Vietnamese guerrillas who fought against the U.S.-backed Saigon regime. Cu Chi was a cobweb of about 120 miles of tunnels about 40 miles from the center of Saigon. The tunnels were often three stories deep, and contained quarters for storage, sleeping and eating, as well as kitchens and rooms for medical operations. The entrances and breathing holes were highly camouflaged, and the system allowed the Viet Cong fighters to appear in and disappear from most areas above ground virtually at will.

The Viet Cong also built booby traps in the same area, examples of which were demonstrated to us. These would be holes dug in the ground and camouflaged. Then when our soldiers stepped on the traps, they would fall upon metal spikes laced with feces that would pierce their feet, or long sharpened poles that would pierce their armpits. There were others that, when triggered, would release metal balls covered with spikes that would swing down upon our soldiers on a vine from a tree. And, of course there were homemade land mines. These traps reflected the realization that the Viet Cong could obtain greater and more lasting psychological advantages by severely injuring our soldiers instead of killing them outright.

Imagine being a U.S. soldier on the ground in this area. In the first place, you couldn't distinguish the friendly Vietnamese from the enemy. And, secondly, imagine being with your best buddy when he had his foot punctured by a metal spike or lost his legs from a land mine. It is not an accident that about one-quarter of all of the disabled homeless people in Orange County are military veterans because many of them experienced these results first hand.

Of course, hundreds of thousands of Viet Cong were killed or injured during our "police action." The conditions in the tunnels alone were terribly unhealthy, with the dampness and the poor air quality caused by oil-burning lamps. And many of the wounded died from infections contracted simply from being underground in the dampness. We also noted that the Viet Cong remolded the metal from the bombs that our forces dropped on them into the spikes for their booby traps, and also that some of the VC would cut some unexploded bombs open so they could reuse the metal and the explosives inside. So one spark and you were history. But all of this vividly brought home to me the commitment of the Viet Cong to kick out what they saw as foreign occupiers, who were first the French, and then the Americans.

While I was stationed with the Navy in Guam from April 1972 until October 1974, I routinely saw large military trucks on our roads carrying 500-pound bombs from the Naval Magazine over to Anderson Air Force Base, where they were loaded onto B-52s. Their motto at Anderson was "Bombs on Target," which is certainly understandable, because that was their job. But I had never before really appreciated the significance of being on the receiving end of a B-52 raid. As we could see at the tunnels area, each bomb left a crater about 30 feet in diameter and about 15 feet deep. Imagine being on the ground or in the tunnels during such a raid!

When we departed Vietnam, I was left with the thought that in many ways North Vietnam would have been far better off had it lost the war to us because then we probably would have poured hundreds of millions of dollars into their country to spur their economy and well-being. They would also have had more freedom, and we would probably now be driving Vietnamese cars. Or, on the other hand, we should have had the courage of our philosophy from the outset and not put in troops in the first place. How so? Because communism simply doesn't work. Our guides in Vietnam routinely said that their country had moved away from communism and over to capitalism exactly for that reason, because once the subsidies from the Soviet Union stopped after its demise, they had no choice. The same thing happened to a major degree in Cambodia and Cuba — and also in China. So today, the Vietnamese government only really runs its oil industry, and, of course, the newspapers and the radio and television stations.

Of course, the communist government in Vietnam committed many human rights atrocities before and after it won the war, and, although the situation is somewhat better, it continues to do so now. Furthermore, although our guides often said there is freedom of speech in Vietnam, reality shows otherwise. And even though the government appears to have the money, it is not spending much of it to address the problems of creating or maintaining the country's infrastructure with regard to paving roads, cleaning water, disposing of trash, and making toilets available. Nevertheless, one way or the other, both sides are worse off because we pursued a military solution.

On the positive side, Vietnam has radically changed for the better in almost every regard. Its government has shifted from taking a highly dogmatic and doctrinaire approach to a more practical one. Vietnam is actively trading goods and services with other countries, and is successfully soliciting investments of foreign capital. With all of that progress, it surprises me that the visa process was so cumbersome and expensive. But these are good signs because only rarely do people shoot their customers, and most investors do not place their money in countries that are not stable.

As a result of this progress, the average wage per person has increased in Vietnam from about $1,000 per year in 1975 to about $2,700 today. Prices are still low there as, for example, an hour's massage cost about $12. But who could have imagined seeing a Mercedes or a Cadillac being driven down the streets of Ho Chi Minh City by a non-government official? We saw quite a few, and that is a revolution all in itself.

Chapter 10

Liberty and Immigration

I seldom get angry at people who are in our country illegally. They are simply doing what our system so strongly encourages them to do, and they almost always come to the United States to seek better lives for themselves and their families, just like our ancestors did. Few people come here to take advantage of us or our welfare system. They come here to work, and they mostly work hard. Instead, I reserve my anger for the so-called immigration system. In this, I am not alone because virtually no one stands up for it. The irony is that it would not be at all difficult to install a program that would work. But seemingly neither the Republicans nor the Democrats want this to happen.

Why not? The answer is money and power. Republicans mostly want to take advantage of the cheap labor presented by "undocumented workers," and Democrats want the votes that will eventually come their way from the increased numbers of people that enter our country. But, in the meantime, many good people are truly suffering and being punished under the status quo. For example, it is quite dangerous and expensive to enter this country illegally, and many workers are exploited by unscrupulous employers once they get here. In addition, we have the unintended consequence that many people here illegally would actually go home after several months if only they felt that they could return later without so much danger and expense. So the present system actually keeps them here longer than they would otherwise stay. In addition, of course, our healthcare, educational, and criminal justice systems have been deeply overburdened by the large numbers of poor, uneducated and unhealthy people who are here illegally.

I, through no effort of my own, was truly blessed to be born in the United States of America. Many people who were not so fortunate have sought to come to this country to pursue a better life for themselves and their children, i.e. to pursue the American Dream, just like me. And they should be allowed to do so! That means that, after a meaningful background check for issues involving things like criminality, mental health and possible terrorist sympathies, any immigrants who can show that they can support themselves should be allowed to live in our country and do so. And if they can support their families, they should be allowed to bring them along.

So why do we perpetuate the present failed system? Because the federal government has virtually all of the power, makes all of the rules and does whatever enforcement that takes place, which is not very much. But the federal government mostly does not have to pay for the costs of those here illegally. Most of those costs are paid by the state and local governments and the school districts. It is time to recognize the legitimate frustration of our state and local governments that are hemorrhaging money to pay for the status quo, but without having any controls whatsoever over those costs. So what is the resolution? Politicians will tell you that the choice is yours: the construction of a wall or, alternatively, open borders. Neither of those proposals will contribute to good results or long-lasting immigration reform.

Arriving at a viable solution reminds me of one of the lessons I learned in law school, which is that the answer to most questions is: it depends. What does that mean? Well, before you can give a reasoned answer to a question, you should know the circumstances and the context in which the question arises. Children often do not understand or employ the "it depends" way of thinking. For them things are usually "all or nothing." But when they mature, they begin to realize that the answers to most questions depend upon the situation, and the risks or benefits of action or inaction. Even though most adults innately do understand this approach, many do not employ it consciously.

One example of where a question cries out for an "it depends" answer is what we should do about our immigration problems. For people to think only in terms of "a wall" or "open borders" is shortsighted in the extreme. The same myopic arguments of all or nothing are being utilized as we navigate police reform in the wake of George Floyd's murder. One side demands we defund the police, without compromise, while the other side wishes to negotiate. The same thing happened when the coronavirus started to spread in U.S. communities. Voices called for a total shutdown, to the detriment of countless businesses, families, and individuals. But the virus didn't spread state-by-state on the same timeline. As a result, newer hotspots delivered regions with a "double whammy:" despite precautionary closures and stay-at-home mandates, places seeking to reopen after months of economic misfortune were hit with substantial spikes in coronavirus cases.

But when you think about it, most issues lend themselves to a similar risk and benefit analysis, as symbolized by the "it depends" answer. That even includes issues about our country's security. For example, should our government be able to wiretap telephone conversations between people here and countries like Libya, Pakistan, and Iran? The answer is (all together now): it depends. What is the threat to our security, and how immediate is that threat? What are the opportunities for the government agents to seek and obtain a judicial warrant? What do our Constitution and judicial precedents say about this situation? In other words, what are the risks and benefits both regarding our security and also regarding our precious liberties?

But there must be some issues that are so clear that the "it depends" answer is not necessary. For example, what about questions concerning the safety of our children? Well, here again it depends upon the situation. Should we not trust any children to cross any street by themselves until they are in high school? That is a certainly a risky activity that can threaten our children's safety, but it still depends upon the situation. What are the ages of the children? What kind of streets are involved, and what are their safety features? These questions should be answered before decisions are made.

Nevertheless, we do not want to descend into moral relativism either. There certainly are some things about which a moral society will not compromise, and in those cases the "it depends" answer does not apply. For example, the answer to questions about slavery, apartheid, the sexual abuse of children, and Hitler's extermination of millions of Jews, gypsies, and others is not "it depends." In my mind there are ambiguities about many or even most issues in the world, but not those. In fact, I will go so far as to say that in some areas there even are even Absolute Right and Absolute Wrong answers, but I may not always be intelligent or perceptive enough to know what those answers should be.

Ultimately, it comes down to drawing from a body of existing and future information to assess an issue, otherwise we risk seeing something other than the full picture. I learned this when I was maybe 5 or 6 years old, when I decided that I didn't need to brush any but my front teeth. What was the rationale for that decision? Because those were the only ones that people saw. But after a few days I encountered additional information when my mouth "felt so yucky," and so I changed my approach. Lesson: decisions are made based upon the information at hand. Thus, the best approach is to get wide-ranging information before making important decisions.

So what does immigration reform look like after applying a cost/benefit analysis with sufficient information? Here's what I found: a fairly straight forward three step process. Of course, there will still be problems, but these changes will allow us in large measure to regain control of our borders, reduce dangers and injustices for non-citizens, seriously reduce the burden upon our taxpayers to support such large numbers of people who are here illegally, reinstitute and reinforce the Rule of Law, bring more employment income back "above the table," and begin to return everybody's lives to normal.

So here are the three steps. First, this failed system will never be changed until the federal government has the incentive to change it. That can be accomplished by requiring the federal government to pay for the governmental costs of people here illegally. Second, we should decide how many people can enter our country to work, and for what period of time they can stay. Then, we should create a workers' program that allows immigrants to have something like an "Orange Card" that will allow them to work here legally during a specified period of time. This would be similar to our former Bracero program and would be in addition to our present resident alien and naturalization programs. And if the workers could support their families, they would be welcome to bring them along. But, other than providing schooling and truly emergency medical care, there would be no welfare involved. But, since they would be here legally, these workers would be able to lead a normal life, obtain driver's licenses, get automobile insurance, pay their taxes, and go back and forth across our borders just like we citizens can.

The third important component of this new program would be to use strict sanctions against all employers who in any way hire workers who are not documented. Thus, those who do not have proper identification would increasingly have trouble finding work, so soon they would probably go elsewhere. In addition, where today many ruffians prey upon people here illegally because they can't call the police and protect themselves, this system would enable them to bring those predators to justice without fear of deportation. And it would also free up our law enforcement officers to chase the bad guys, instead of chasing working families. So, once again, I ask, what's not to like?

Holding people who hire undocumented workers responsible for their illegal acts would be the key, but it can be done. With today's computer-chip technology, we should easily be able to create an identification card that cannot be forged. So there would be no excuse for hiring people who do not have such a card. And once we have a workable system for identification, we could also exclude permanently from admission to the country those immigrants who persist in violating our laws.

By adopting this approach, not only would we be upholding a human liberty, we would also bring large beneficial results for our economy. Why? Because if labor is not allowed to go to capital, capital will go to labor. And it is better for our economic prosperity for businesses to be located in our country than elsewhere. So in this area, like so many others, Liberty continues to work!

And then, there is the question about whether the 14th Amendment should confer automatic citizenship upon all babies born within our borders. The applicable language cited for that result is: "All persons born or naturalized in the United States and subject to the jurisdiction thereof, are citizens of the United States..." Up until now, this provision has been interpreted to stand for automatic citizenship. But the interpretation should be re-examined. As you will recall from your history classes, the 14th Amendment was passed in July of 1868, after the Civil War had ended, and it was intended to confer citizenship upon former slaves. But the framers of the amendment simply could not stop with the words "all persons," because when the Constitution was ratified, slaves were officially recognized only to be 3/5 of a person. Thus, additional language was needed to address those former slaves.

Nevertheless, if the framers of that amendment were here today and asked whether they meant to confer automatic citizenship upon a baby who, for example, was on an airplane flying from Mexico City to Toronto, but was born while the plane was refueling in St. Louis, they would give you a four-word response, which would be: "What, are you crazy?" And they would also give you the same answer if asked about children born in our country to parents who were here illegally.

Then, after pondering the situation a bit further, the framers would say: "Wait a minute, we already addressed these issues in the amendment itself by inserting the clause 'subject to the jurisdiction thereof.' If we had meant literally anyone born here would become a citizen, we would have left that clause out!"

And that is the answer. If a citizen of Japan is arrested here while on vacation, he doesn't call our embassy; he calls the Japanese embassy because he is still subject to the jurisdiction of Japan even though his physical presence is here. Thus, the 14th Amendment does not need to be amended, just correctly interpreted. Re-interpretation is certainly not something to be done lightly, but it has happened before. For example, in Brown v. Board of Education in 1954, the U.S. Supreme Court reversed the 1896 precedent of Plessy v. Ferguson by holding that "separate but equal" public schools were not equal and were therefore unconstitutional. In a similar fashion, the Supreme Court should re-examine the 14th Amendment.

It is time to do away with our present failed immigration system. Of course, there will still be problems, but these changes will allow us in large measure to regain control of our borders, reduce dangers and injustices for the foreign workers, seriously reduce the burden upon our taxpayers to support such large numbers of people who are here illegally, reinstitute and reinforce the Rule of Law, and begin to return our lives back to normal.

Only after we have a system in place to control our borders should we address the difficult and emotional problem of who receives "amnesty" or citizenship and who does not, and how to institute that in relationship to those people who have followed our laws and regulations and have requested to enter our great country through proper channels.

Many people have complained that President Trump has wrongly set aside some of President Obama's "good works," regarding things like DACA, which have kept people who were brought into our country as small children without complying with our immigration laws from being deported. But the problem does not lie with Trump, it actually lies with Obama and Congress. Why? Because Mr. Obama issued Executive Orders for our laws not to be enforced for those young people. So, that being the case, no one has a legitimate complaint when Trump similarly issues Executive Orders repealing them. But if President Obama had respected the process and successfully attempted to have the immigration laws changed, President Trump would have been forced to do the same.

In other words, the process is critically important. We don't have dictators in our country who can rule by fiat — or by Presidential Executive Order. The DACA issue to me is clear: we should keep those young people who have adapted well into our society here, and I believe most Americans would agree with that result. So the Rule of Law should be respected, such that Congress should vote to modify our immigration laws to enact that result. But this is yet another example of Congress abrogating its lawmaking responsibilities to a president.

There's another harsh reality: most politicians (and voters) are outcome oriented, which means that they often first make up their minds about what their goals are and then try thereafter to justify those outcomes with doctrinal support. Accordingly, when politicians are out of power nationally, they tend to support the 10th Amendment, but when they are in power, they tend to ignore it. As I hope (probably in vain) that everyone knows, the 10th Amendment expressly provides that all powers not delegated by the Constitution to the federal government are reserved to the States and to the People.

So, for example, conservatives argued during the Clinton Administration that the federal government could not command the states to enforce a federal regulatory gun control program. The feds could try to enforce it themselves, if they so choose, but the states could not be commanded to cooperate (see the 1997 United States Supreme case of Printz v. United States). But now that conservatives are in power, liberals are now "seeing the light" and arguing that the 10th Amendment supports their establishment of so-called "sanctuary cities," where the feds cannot command state and local governments to cooperate with the federal government's immigration programs.

Liberty is consistent and agrees with both arguments. In fact, Liberty would expand them to cover the federal government's inability to command state and local governments to help enforce federal marijuana laws. The Supreme Court has made it clear that federal law can prohibit marijuana under the commerce clause (see the wrongly decided case of Angel Raich v. Ashcroft), but it still cannot command the states to help enforce those federal laws.

As Justice Scalia said in Printz, the federal commandeering of state governments goes against the text, structure, and history of the Constitution. So, if we are to be true to our Constitution — and to our principles — we will enforce the provisions of the 10th Amendment regardless of who is in power. Without question, our Founders disagreed upon many things, and often were forced to compromise on many of them. But, without exception, each of the 55 delegates to the 1787 Constitutional Convention agreed that the most important duty of government was to protect individual liberties from encroachment by government! (The second-most important was to keep us safe.) As a result, most of them felt that the Constitution was so clear on this point that the 10th Amendment was unnecessary because it would have been redundant. Once again, that doesn't mean that the federal government cannot attempt to enforce its laws on its own. But it does mean that the states cannot be commanded to enforce laws with which they do not agree. That is a fundamental freedom set forth in our Constitution, and the Founders are depending upon us, for our own Liberty, to honor it!

Chapter 11

Liberty and Religion

Before I met and married wonderful wife, Grace, I belonged to the Garden Grove Methodist Church. Some years ago, I was asked to give a sermon there. I was truly proud and happy to do so, but I then had to figure out what to speak about. So if you have an opportunity to give a sermon on a topic of your own choosing in church, what would you discuss?

Well, I reflected for a while on the subject, and eventually landed on a theme: "We are Christians. Does it make any difference?" Of course, there are significant differences because of Christian theology, and the story and teachings of Jesus. But are there any other differences as well? And if there are, what are they? See if your answers are the same as mine.

I began my sermon by saying that I recently had published a book on judging in an attempt to pass along to new judges any wisdom I had gathered from my 25 years on the bench. And the first sentence of the preface of that book said that the best decision I had ever made in my life was choosing my parents. Of course, the benefits of that "choice" had made enormous differences in my life. My parents were a huge support system, and they provided me with love that was both unconditional and unending.

I confess that sometimes I had put that love to the test. For example, when I was 10 years old, I once attempted to shoplift a bag of Tootsie Rolls from a local market. But I got caught, and then was forced to inform my parents. They stood by me without recrimination, but I could tell that they were as disappointed in me as I was in myself. Since that time, I have never again stolen anything from anybody — and I also have not been able to look another bag of Tootsie Rolls in the face!

But what a gift my parents gave me with this love and support! Of course, I believe that those gifts also came with a moral obligation to help those people on this Earth who did not "choose" their parents quite so well. Like me, most people at least originally became Christians only by accident of birth. Thereafter, many people actually focus on the teachings of Jesus, weigh the Christian theology against that of other religions, and then choose to continue to follow the Christian faith or not. But many people did not choose to stay as Christians any more than I actually chose my parents. In fact, if their parents had been Hindu, the odds are overwhelming that they would still be Hindu to this day.

Did God choose us? Well, I certainly do not know the answer to that question because it is "well above my pay grade." But I do know that God did give us choices in life and then, just like my parents, is proud when we choose well, and disappointed when we choose poorly. But He still loves us regardless of the choices we make, without condition and without end. And that is a difference, in fact a big one.

Like many other people, I have tried to live the type of life that would allow me to be satisfied when I looked back on it from my deathbed, just as St. Peter does as we try to enter the Pearly Gates. So, if I could give myself some advice from that position at the end of my life, it would be three things. First, love the people who treat you right, and absolutely forget about those who don't. Second, if you get a chance in life, take it! In that regard, try to make the lyrics of the song "I'm Gonna Live Till I Die" be your motto. "Until my number's up, I'm gonna fill my cup / I'm gonna live, live, live until I die." And third, treat people like people. I have already related to you the story about my father treating the custodians in federal court as important individuals, so I won't repeat it. But it was in my sermon.

On this subject, I recommend you read the book, *The Anatomy of Peace* by the Arbinger Institute. This well-crafted and easy-reading book discusses the difference between treating another person as a person, or as an object. If we treat others as people, we do not need to justify our own prejudices, depressions, self-righteousness or fears, because those issues simply don't arise. But if we treat them as objects, all of these harmful and degrading traits within us often increase and harden, which will in turn allow them to poison us. Then we proceed to use the injustices that are done to us as justifications to do further injustices to others. At that point, we become our own enemies by using our mistreatments to destroy our own peace. So it is not just the dictators of some nations of the world that inflict bad things upon others in order to get or maintain power. All of us can do that as well.

Jesus said: "If you love me, then feed my sheep." With the blessings we have received, we can help administer to the needs of others who, often through nothing they have done, are not as fortunate as we are. I think that is the answer. Oh, I know that we can't bring peace to the whole world, and it may be naïve to believe otherwise. But we can bring peace to our world! Like the hymn says, "Let there be peace on Earth, and let it begin with me."

We are truly blessed. We have chosen well or, one way or the other, we were eternally lucky to have been chosen. Our Father loves us, without condition, and without end. He cares about us, and wants to be proud of us. It matters, and what a difference it makes! So, in the time remaining to us upon this earth, we should stand up extra straight. Walk proud. And fear not. Because we are Christians. We are living our lives nestled in the arms of a loving God!

My wife Grace and I went on a two-week trip in 2011 to Jordan and Israel sponsored by Saint Michael & All Angels Episcopal Church in Corona del Mar, California. What a great trip, and what a privilege to visit places I have read about in the Bible and elsewhere since childhood. It was truly sobering to think that we were standing in the places where so many important things happened throughout history. As one of my best friends says, the Holy Land is a powerful place filled with confusion, but it brings clarity to pilgrims seeking to know God. I agree and, first and foremost, this was a humbling religious experience. But it was so intensely personal that I don't feel I can share it with you, other than to ask you to pray for me, as I will pray for you.

Otherwise, as St. Augustine said, "Life is a book, and people who don't travel read only one page." In that regard, there were many things I had not realized before this trip, such as how small Israel is. For example, the distance from Jerusalem to Bethlehem is about five miles, to Jericho about 40 miles, and to Nazareth about 70.

Furthermore, and I don't think this is sacrilegious, often throughout our time in the Holy Land, I kept wondering why God would have ever designated this place as the "Promised Land," where it is hot, dry, and rocky. Why not Maui, Pacific Palisades, or Newport Beach instead? We started in Petra, Jordan, one of the great historic archeological sites. The elaborate tombs of kings and nobles were sculpted straight out of the sandstone cliffs. (And I am happy to tell you that Petra was not destroyed by Indiana Jones in his "Last Crusade" movie.) We also visited the Sea of Galilee, which is really a freshwater lake, and swam in the Dead Sea, which is the lowest point on Earth's surface at 1,400 feet below sea level, and is so salty that it probably is impossible to drown. In fact, I couldn't even sit down in 18 inches of water because my legs kept popping up.

The ruins of the synagogue at Capernaum on the Sea of Galilee were truly moving. This was where Jesus spent most of his time teaching, where he gathered disciples, and also performed some of his miracles. We also learned that, as best as can be determined, actual history does not match some of the stories we have heard all of our lives. For example, Jesus was probably born in 4 B.C., around harvest time, which would have been in April instead of December. And there probably weren't any "inns" as we think of them in Bethlehem. Instead, there were numerous caves, some of which were reserved for people living communally, and others were left for the animals. So, actually, the innkeeper in the Christmas story has probably been wrongly disparaged throughout history, because, by providing the space in a cave with the animals, he was giving Mary some privacy during childbirth, which she otherwise would not have had.

And because they had little wood in the area, what we call the manger was probably a stone watering trough for the animals. But although these variances are interesting intellectually, they certainly do not make any difference in the religious significance of the stories. Another place that really had an impact on me was the fairly new Basilica of the Annunciation in Nazareth, which was built near the site where the Archangel Gabriel informed Mary that she had been chosen to bear the Son of God. Within the basilica are large and deeply impressive murals from many countries of the world depicting the impact of that wonderful story from their perspective. My favorite murals were from South Africa, Japan, and the United States.

But the most overwhelming experience was being inside the Old City of Jerusalem, where we followed the Stations of the Cross on the Via Dolorosa, and went to the Church of the Holy Sepulcher. Being in the places where Jesus bore the cross, and was crucified, died, placed in a tomb, and resurrected was beyond deeply moving and sobering. It really cannot be explained, but only experienced.

Although I am not Jewish, the Western Wall was also a place of deep impact. Their belief is that God is actually always present at this, the nearest point to the destroyed Temple. And the people praying at this wall with such sincere devotion is something worthy of the utmost respect. In fact, I literally perceived them as talking directly to God!

During my time there, I felt safe and even welcomed. But this certainly is a deeply troubled land where the Palestinians are obviously being occupied, and the evidence of past and present conflict is never far away. Throughout Israel are young men and women in the police or army, both Israeli and Palestinian, armed with machine guns. At the River Jordan, we saw portable bridges that could be used by the army immediately in the event the bridges were destroyed.

And, of course, the tilt-up, 25-foot high cement wall in Jerusalem separating the Palestinian from the Israeli land, along with the armed checkpoints through it, were omnipresent scars. As a professional mediator of disputes, it continually went through my mind that all of this should be unnecessary.

If people would begin by understanding that there are no "solutions" to these problems that go back for hundreds and even thousands of years, that would be a good start. Instead there are only "resolutions," which will not be perfect, but the best that can be achieved under difficult circumstances.

Israelis should be ensured of their right to exist safely in their own land; Palestinians should have a designated country of their own, and be able to control their own water, power, and movements; and all religious sites should be respected and as much as possible be under the control of the group that is affected by them. Fortunately, the Palestinians now seem to be closer to having a responsible government with whom the Israelis and others can negotiate. The U.S. should step forward and exert some neutral and principled leadership to help bring a lasting peace to this confused place. Probably no one else could do it but us, and it is long since time for us to take that role.

So, does it matter? I wondered while pondering how to address the Garden Grove Methodist Church. Does it make a difference that we are Christians? The question led me to recall a discussion I had at the same St. Michael's Church about the importance of the separation of church and state. This subject can be considered controversial because some people consider that it could be seen as an attack on religion. But I simply do not agree with that assessment.

I view this separation as being one of the most important war-and-peace issues of the 21st century. Of course, there will be some exceptions, but in general governments that maintain the separation of church and state will be far less likely to be involved in war than those that do not. For example, we all should be concerned today about the governments of Pakistan, Iran, Afghanistan and others where religion plays a large part in the affairs of government.

Although we generally consider separation of church and state to be addressed in our Constitution, it is not really all that clear. The 1st Amendment specifies that Congress shall make no law respecting the establishment of religion or the free exercise thereof, but that could be read as only controlling the actions of Congress, not those of individuals or churches.

The most-cited reference to the separation doctrine comes from a letter written by Thomas Jefferson in 1802, well after the Constitution was ratified, to the Danbury Baptist Association of Connecticut. In this letter, Jefferson said that there must be a "wall of separation between church and state." Nevertheless, the 1st Amendment was later interpreted by the United States Supreme Court as forbidding anyone from bringing religion into government, and vice versa.

This is considered an important issue because of the two goals connected to it. The first is to protect government from the undue influence of religious organizations. That is not to say that governments cannot be influenced by religious values, and it also does not imply that we should become a secular society. That is not even a part of the discussion, nor should it be! But if you look back into the history of our country, you will find that churches strongly influenced the Salem Witch Trials. Elsewhere, you will find similar tragic results with the Spanish Inquisition, the Crusades, and the Holy Roman Empire. That is not to say we are in imminent peril; but it is simply to say that we should be aware that the seeds are there.

Similarly, the Catholic Church in the 1600s caused Galileo to be prosecuted for proposing the scientific belief that the Earth rotated around the sun. This is not an untypical response when churches have some controls over governments and people attempt to question church dogma. Again the seeds are there as well for the suppression of such an inquiry.

More recently we have seen the accusations against China, of operating mass detention centers, or "re-education camps" targeting Uyghurs and other Muslims. Once in custody, the goal is to indoctrinate them with normative beliefs. The argument is that this contributes to counter movements of terrorism and extremism. That is blatant religious persecution. And then, we see the inverse: rules in the name of God where, for example, governments require women to cover themselves with scarves and burqas or countenance the stoning of women for perceived sexual or other transgressions. Religion is often corrupting of government, and it should be kept separate.

Furthermore, it is not hard for one person or a small group of people to accumulate a large amount of power and influence in a church. Most churches are designed that way, with examples being the pope in Rome, and the ayatollahs in Iran. No one should want church officials to become in any way in charge of civilian governments. Besides, probably anyone who does not see the problem can almost immediately be helped to see the light by being asked the following question: How would you feel if the other guy's religion is chosen to lead or have undue influence on your government? I think we all know the answer.

If our country were to choose to have a state religion, or even be strongly influenced by a particular one, a conservative Christian religion would probably be selected. But, in reality, it is too late. We have long since also become a nation of Jews, Hindus, Muslims, less conservative Christian religions, and many other religions, as well as people who are atheists, humanists, or who have no religion at all. And if those people felt that someone else's beliefs were going to have undue influence with their own government, it could very well lead to a civil war. Why? Because they are Americans too and would rightly not want formally to be discriminated against by their own government.

However, some Christian fundamentalists openly argue that governments in America must come under the control of religious leaders like them. With many of these people, there are often only two camps: Good and Evil, and they preach that not to be firm in what they define as "good" would be evil so as to tempt God's disfavor and wrath.

This Christian fundamentalist movement has been greatly assisted by the increasing polarization of the people in our country. For example, I originally welcomed the coming of cable television with its large numbers of channels because I thought this would expose people to more varied points of view. But now, I see that the reverse has actually occurred. Most of these channels cater their reporting and editorial comments to people who already have a fixed outlook and philosophy, and those people mostly only watch those stations. So this results in these people's established views only getting more reinforced.

Aside from the concern that Christian religious fundamentalists could take us back to the mentality of the Spanish Inquisition or the Salem Witch Trials, the time has long-since passed that we can become a nation officially dominated by Christianity, or any other religion. One of the significant reasons is that at this point we have large numbers of Jews, Muslims, Hindus, Buddhists, atheists, and others who rightfully see America as their country too, and the likelihood that they would respond violently if they were to be officially subjected to Christian or any other religious doctrines and dictates would be substantial.

To guard against this potential result, we must stand firm in sponsoring a government that accommodates the free but peaceful exercise of one's chosen religion, whatever it may be, if any. But if we ever allow religious "errors," misstatements or even tastelessness to be prosecuted or even prohibited, we will be on the road to facing the same type of problems that exist in some of these Muslim countries.

So in matters of religion, government must be strictly neutral. People must be able to choose for themselves, even if they choose "badly." If particular religious doctrines are "right," they will win people's hearts and minds in the free marketplace of ideas. But as soon as a government takes sides and starts to enforce one interpretation of religious "rightness" over another, religious zealotry will not be far behind. And soon thereafter will come violence, chaos, war, and the loss of the America that we know and love.

In addition, and this could be misunderstood (and realistically some people will do so intentionally), all "hate crimes" should be repealed as being counterproductive. Why? Because if a law says that an assault based upon your race, sexual orientation, religion, etc. is a special or distinctive crime, then I — in most cases justifiably — will feel that an assault based upon my race, sexual orientation, religion, etc. should be seen a special or distinctive crime too! In addition, and as a practical matter, where can the line be drawn? An assault upon an Asian or a Buddhist? How about an assault upon an Italian, or someone that is Italian but for some reason looks Asian? Or upon someone who is simply thinking of converting to Buddhism? The problems and complications will never end!

Even though it is undeniably true that our society has done and has even institutionally sanctioned some bad things to some people, like slavery, segregation, and various other laws of prohibition, simply because of their race, sexual orientation, or religion, the better approach in this complicated and multifaceted world is to realize that an assault is a crime. Of course, some are more serious than others. If the offense is distinctively offensive for reasons based upon race, sexual orientation, or religion, etc., or anything else, that can — and should — be explicitly addressed at the sentencing phase of the proceedings. But Liberty dictates that no one person by law should be deemed to be more special or distinctive than any other. And, once again, by following the dictates of Liberty, we will not be required to pass so many laws, and we will also avoid a lot of legitimately hurt feelings.

So what about "In God We Trust" on our currency, or "Under God" in our Pledge of Allegiance? Are those unconstitutional? Actually not, because, fortunately, the courts have understood that these are a large part of who we are and an expression that, from the Founders on up until today, we are generally a "God-Fearing People," and that we trust and believe in God. The same thing is true for us to continue to celebrate Christmas as a national holiday, or for religious events or servants like Mother Teresa to be celebrated on our postage stamps. Of course, there will be those who try to "push the envelope" on both sides of those issues. But, again, fortunately, the courts have seen it appropriate to celebrate and maintain the historical and traditional parts of our nation.

By analogy, aspirin probably would not be cleared today by the Food and Drug Administration, because it can be used in a dangerous if not life-threatening fashion. But we have grown up with it, it is a part of us and our culture, and there is virtually no chance that it will be recalled or even more heavily controlled. Nor should it be. But had the phrase on our money been "In Jesus We Trust," or the pledge instead contained "One Nation under Buddha," that would appropriately have been held to violate the Constitution and the doctrine of the separation of church and state.

The second critical goal is to enforce this separation for the protection of churches from the undue influence of government. When my wife Grace and I took our fabulous trip to Turkey, we learned that the government actually pays much of the salaries of the imams, who are the Muslim prayer leaders. When I asked why, our guide simply said that this was an effective way for the government to exercise some control over the actions of the religious leaders. Obviously, these religious leaders would have a tendency to ease back on their criticism of the same entity that was issuing their paychecks. But the danger to religious freedom under those circumstances is obvious.

Similarly, we should be quite concerned about our government funneling charitable funds through religious institutions. It sounds fine in concept for the government to fund wonderful organizations like the Salvation Army and church-sponsored food kitchens for the poor, but remember that where government money is given, control is sure to follow. And then the "strings" attached to the funding invariably become ropes and chains. So in many ways it would be better for the money to be funneled to non-religious organizations. Besides, if the government funds your religious group's charities, why shouldn't it also fund mine? And that only begins the friction, because one person's charity can quickly become another person's terrorist group. Those conflicts will never end, so it is better not to get started down that road in the first place.

Finally, and as importantly, by enforcing the Separation of Church and State, we will not only protect government from religious zealotry, but we will also be protecting religion from governmental zealotry as well. So in the long run, religion and government will both win, and the world will also be more likely to be at peace. And, as Shakespeare would say, that is "devoutly to be wished."

Chapter 12

Liberty and the War on Drugs*

I am a former "drug warrior." Although I may not have given it too much critical thought, during my time of service in the U.S. Navy JAG Corps and as a federal prosecutor in the U.S. Attorney's Office in Los Angeles, I believed that people using and possessing illicit drugs rightfully should be in jail. In fact, I was probably raised just like you were, which was to equate cocaine and heroin with bad, with evil, and with prison.

But then I was appointed as a trial court judge in Orange County, California by Governor Deukmejian at the end of 1983. Once on the bench my views slowly began to change. I began to realize that we were not doing anything positive for low-level drug offenders. All we were doing was churning them through the system, and at great human and financial cost. I also began to realize that when we arrested drug sellers it really did not make any difference in the overall availability of drugs, because other drug dealers or potential drug dealers simply treated the situation as a new job opportunity.

---

* This chapter was first published in *The Chapman Law Review*, Volume 13, Spring, 2010.

If I can trace my change of thinking back to any particular epiphany, it was when I was presiding over a felony preliminary hearing calendar and was taking a plea and delivering a sentence that another judge had agreed upon for a juvenile who was being tried and sentenced as an adult. This seventeen-year-old hoodlum was pleading guilty to the offenses of assaulting and raping prostitutes and then robbing them of their money. But the sentence he would be receiving, when giving him credit for some jail time he had already served, resulted in him being released from custody in less than two weeks.

So I listened while the young defendant provided a "factual basis" to show that he was guilty of the offenses, made sure he understood his constitutional rights and desired to waive them, and then gave him the agreed-upon sentence. All during this time, he was quite respectful, of course, as most defendants are before a sentence is pronounced. But once the matter was concluded and as he was being led back into the holding cell, he let out a "war whoop" because he was so pleased with the outcome.

At that moment, I realized the truth, which is that he had in fact won because we are spending so much of our public resources on cases involving non-violent drug offenders that we do not have enough resources left effectively to pursue other righteous cases involving things like assaults, rapes, robberies, murders, and frauds. In other words, the "tougher" we get on drug crimes, literally the "softer" we get in the prosecution of everything else. That conclusion was subsequently reinforced when I read of an investigation by the Los Angeles Times, which disclosed that only about forty-seven percent of all homicides between the years 1990-1994 were even prosecuted, compared with about eighty percent in the late 1960s. Why was that?

The answer is that we were too busy prosecuting non-violent drug offenders. So, as I began to open my eyes further to these realities, I decided to share my conclusions with as many people as I could.

As a result, on April 8, 1992, I did something quite unusual for a sitting trial court judge. I took a half-day vacation, held a press conference in the plaza behind our courthouse, and recommended that we legalize all drugs. The press conference was successful in getting my opinions out to the public, and I have been actively involved in publicly discussing this critical issue ever since that time. In fact, the writing of this book is simply a continuation of that effort.

Most sophisticated people understand that life can be complicated, and that it is filled with distinctions. But, to our great detriment, for the most part neither our community nor our governments have understood, recognized, or even discussed some critically important distinctions regarding the important area of drug policy. So, for me to relay those distinctions to you, I'll start by answering a seemingly simple question: what is a drug?

Yes, it is true that aspirin and penicillin are drugs, but those are not what we are discussing here. Instead, for these purposes, I suggest that we are discussing mind-altering and sometimes-addicting substances. And what are some of these substances? Heroin, cocaine, and methamphetamines quickly come to mind. There are also other natural substances like mushrooms, peyote, and other hallucinogens, plus chemical substances like LSD, PCP, ecstasy, and various designer drugs, which also fit the description. Marijuana is also often included on that list, but some people argue that it is not physiologically addicting. But is that all? No, and here is another place where our nation's drug policy has broken down. Other highly available mind-altering and sometimes-addicting substances must also be included in our policy, such as alcohol, nicotine, and even caffeine.

I use alcohol and, decreasingly, caffeine, and so do most other adults I know, and lots of people smoke cigarettes. So why should those substances be included in our National Drug Control Policy? I understand that they are not used as often as the others just to "separate from reality," and I am certainly not saying that we should make them illegal. But just because these drugs are legal does not at all mean that they cannot also produce many of the same harms as illegal drugs.

Of course, if our societal goal were to protect people from the greatest killer drug of all in this area that the user could take, then we would make tobacco illegal. Every year more than 400,000 people die in our country alone because they use tobacco. To his lasting credit, C. Everett Koop, the U.S. Surgeon General under President Ronald Reagan, was the first person successfully to spread the alarm about the harms of using tobacco. He used that figure to explain the extent of the danger, but found that it did not have much of an impact. Instead he analogized it to be the same as if two jumbo jets filled with passengers were to crash and burn every day, killing everyone aboard. That is the number of people that die each year in our country because they use tobacco.

So why not make cigarettes illegal? Simply because that act would bring in, and in many ways create, the "Al Capones" and other gangsters in our world who would quickly satisfy the demand for cigarettes, along with all of the accompanying violence, corruption, and lack of respect for the law. Fortunately, we all seem to realize that this would not be an effective "remedy," and that it would also make criminals almost overnight out of the millions of people who are addicted to cigarettes who would continue to use them.

To the contrary, our approach to tobacco usage has been a remarkable success story. Our efforts at honest education have resulted in the material decrease of tobacco usage and, by regulating the locations where people can smoke, we have significantly reduced the irritation and harms of "second-hand smoke" to non-smokers. Probably no laws of prohibition could have ever obtained these positive results.

The second biggest killer of the users of mind-altering and sometimes-addicting drugs is alcohol. Approximately 88,000 people in our country die every year because they use this substance. They die from things like cirrhosis of the liver, alcohol hepatitis, and kidney failure. Of course, we tried to reduce those numbers by making alcohol illegal with the passage of the Eighteenth Amendment, which went into effect in January 1920. But, after an initial decrease in alcohol usage, by the time Alcohol Prohibition was finally repealed with the passage of the Twenty-first Amendment in 1933, alcohol usage had returned to its initial rate.

Of course, during Alcohol Prohibition we also saw a significant increase in crime, violence, corruption, disrespect for the law, as well as, critically, death from poisoned liquor (the "bathtub gin" problem). In addition, we also observed firsthand the "Cardinal Rule of Prohibition," which is "always push the sale of the stronger stuff." To explain, if bootleggers face the same criminal justice sanctions for selling a barrel of beer as they would for selling a barrel of whiskey, which will they sell? The answer to that question is easy. They will sell the whiskey because they can make about three to four times more money by selling the stronger stuff. That same reality exists just as strongly today, thus drug dealers push cocaine and methamphetamines upon our children, who often would prefer only to smoke marijuana or take ecstasy at dance parties.

But why should caffeine be a part of our nation's drug policy? Is caffeine a "good drug" or a "bad drug?" Actually, caffeine is a stimulant to the central nervous system that in massive dosages can be lethal. Of course, caffeine can also increase alertness, but it can also reduce fine motor skills. It can also cause insomnia, headaches, nervousness, and dizziness. It can also constrict blood vessels, relax air passages to improve breathing, and allow some muscles to contract more easily. In other words, caffeine is just a "thing," and it can have both harmful as well as beneficial effects.

So shouldn't the effects of caffeine on adults be studied and disseminated? As an example, are you aware that the name for Coca-Cola was not a coincidence? Cocaine was an ingredient in that product from 1886-1900. Of course, the cocaine probably had nothing to do with the flavor or the formula; instead it was likely only added to cause people to become addicted to the product so the manufacturer would be able to sell more product. But when people eventually discovered what was in it, they were so upset that the manufacturers took it out. And what did they replace it with? Caffeine, which was probably added for exactly the same reasons as was the cocaine.

What are the effects of caffeine upon pregnant women, or upon children, whose bodies are developing? Today caffeine in soft drinks is aggressively marketed to young children. So can that be harmful to them? Mostly we do not know because our nation's drug policy has not promoted research or disseminated information in that area. This should definitely be changed!

And what about the hypocrisy today as seen in our actions between "good" drugs as opposed to "bad" drugs? Our children see their parents decry the usage of "drugs" on the one hand, and then do not hesitate to give their teenage daughter a valium to calm her down when the "boy of her dreams" asks some other young lady to the prom. They also watch their parents have a couple of stiff drinks to "unwind" when they come home from work. And they see how President Bill Clinton's comments (with a wink) that he smoked marijuana but he "didn't inhale" have turned into a lasting national joke. In addition, they see former Vice President Al Gore as being opposed to the use of marijuana even for medical purposes, yet as being considered to have smoked marijuana regularly when he was a young newspaper reporter in the early 1970s. They even hear of allegations that former President George W. Bush himself used cocaine when he was younger, a discussion that he deflected by saying that the past is the past.

Of course, that did not stop Mr. George W. Bush, when he was the Governor of Texas, from signing a 1997 bill that required anyone possessing a gram or more of cocaine, even for the first time, to serve a minimum of 180 days in jail. On the other hand, President Barack Obama openly admitted in one of his books that he used marijuana and even cocaine when he was in high school and college. Yet there was no general outcry that this has made him incapable of being our nation's president because of those acts, even though many hundreds of thousands of people in our country have been imprisoned for the identical conduct. As a result of all of this hypocrisy, how can people be surprised when our children do not take us or our laws in this area seriously? A material change in our nation's drug policy would be a material change away from hypocrisy.

In addition, there's another important distinction: drug harm as opposed to drug money harm. The reality is that our attempts to rid our world of illicit drugs have indisputably failed. In other words, these drugs, dangerous as they can be, are here to stay. But we should not be surprised at that fact because there has never been a civilization in the history of mankind that has not had some form of mind-altering and sometimes-addicting drugs to use, misuse, abuse, and get addicted to — except the Eskimos because they couldn't grow anything. But now modern chemistry and transportation have changed that reality.

So instead, think of it this way: In many ways we couldn't make these drugs more available if we tried. For example, several years ago Charles Manson was transferred from Corcoran State Prison in California to another facility because he was found to be selling illicit drugs from his prison cell — and he was in solitary confinement! How could this happen? The answer is that there is so much money to be made by smuggling drugs into prisons that lots of people, including prison guards, simply cannot resist the temptation of selling or smuggling small amounts of drugs for large amounts of money. So, if we cannot keep these drugs out of our prisons — and we cannot — what makes us think we can keep them off the streets of any of our towns or cities?

Without a doubt, these drugs can be dangerous. Never once have I heard of anyone saying or even implying that being a heroin addict is a good thing. But our great country is actually facing two problems in this area. One is "drug harm," and that is certainly a substantial problem. But the other is "drug money harm." I am convinced that if reasonable people would simply use their own experiences and observations to reflect upon this matter, they would be as convinced as I am that drug money harms are far costlier in every way than the drug harms ever could be.

All neutral studies in the last 100 years that have been undertaken either by government commissions or by private foundations in Great Britain, Canada, and the United States have reached that same conclusion. They all generally recommend that we go away from the criminal justice approach and adopt what they usually call "drug decriminalization," because of all of the benefits that would accrue from that change. The studies expressly make this recommendation "even if that approach would result in increased drug usage."

Over the years, I myself sentenced several burglars who, at the time of sentencing, told me variations of the following: "Your Honor, three months ago I realized that I was a cocaine addict with a $200-per-day habit. So I went to a drug treatment facility and asked for some help. They had me fill out a bunch of forms and then they told me to come back in six months, because they didn't have the money." Do you realize how much of our property a burglar would have to steal to support a $200-per-day habit? Since a "fence" for the stolen property will only give someone about ten percent of its value, those burglars had to steal about $2,000 per day just to support their habits!

Of course, we will not spend the $2,000-$3,000 per year for outpatient drug treatment that might help them (and significantly reduce crime along the way), but we will spend the $70,000 to $80,000 per year without hesitation to put them in jail or prison.

As a result of this shortsighted approach, the United States leads the world in the incarceration of its people — both in sheer numbers and per capita. We have about five percent of the world's population, but we have about twenty-five percent of its prisoners. As of the year

2007, the United States had 2.3 million people behind bars. China, which has four times our population, was in a distant second place with 1.6 million prisoners — although I agree that this does not include hundreds of thousands of "political activists" who are in "detention."

That means that we have 751 people behind bars for every 100,000 population (if you count only adults, 1,000 for every 100,000 population). Russia, with 627 for every 100,000 population, is the only major industrialized nation that comes anywhere close to us. England's rate is 151; Germany's is 88; Japan's is only 63. These statistics led James Q. Whitman, who is a specialist in comparative law at Yale, to write, "Far from serving as a model for the world, contemporary America is viewed with horror."

In almost every way, this situation and these numbers are the result of drug money harm, not drug harm. Because illicit drugs are so expensive, many drug users and particularly addicts are forced to commit crimes in order to get money to purchase the drugs. This results in many house and vehicle burglaries, check offenses, robberies at automatic teller machines and, certainly, prostitution. It also directly results in the violence by illicit drug dealers to "protect their fiefdoms" from other dealers, or to "convince" their drug-using customers to get the money to pay past debts for their expensive purchases.

To address this reality in economic terms, criminalizing a product necessarily reduces the supply, which then substantially increases the price. That, in turn, makes it more lucrative for people to risk even large criminal justice sanctions to sell the prohibited product. This directly results in increased crime both because the users must obtain the increased amount of money to purchase the product, and because the illegal dealers must use even more violence and threats of violence to protect their now more valuable market from other dealers. So all of this harmful activity is pre-ordained, and all of our efforts to repeal the Law of Supply and Demand are destined to be unsuccessful. Yet we still express surprise at the results!

Actually, none of these drugs are expensive to grow, manufacture, package, or distribute. Marijuana is not called a "weed" for nothing — it will grow anywhere. And, contrary to the attempts of the DEA to persuade us to the contrary, the opium poppy used to make heroin does not need a "mountainous" climate to grow and flourish. For years, this beautiful flower was grown by the National Park Service at Thomas Jefferson's home in Monticello, until the DEA ordered its removal. So if the poppies will grow in Virginia, they would grow virtually anywhere.

The rise in our prison population is also the natural result of the growth of bureaucracies. Once a bureaucracy is in place, its natural inclination is to grow and to justify its own existence. Among other things, that takes the form of increasing arrests of non-violent marijuana users. For example, an annual FBI report that was released at the end of 2007 showed that marijuana arrests had climbed in each of the four preceding years. In the year 2006, there actually were 829,627 state and local arrests for marijuana, and a full eighty-nine percent of those were only for possession, not for its sale or manufacture. That means that there was one marijuana arrest in our country every thirty-eight seconds! And, strongly believe on balance, most of them did far more harm than good.

So the question must be asked, just because some people make a stupid mistake and use, or even get themselves addicted to, some of these drugs, why should I suffer? Why must I put bars on my windows and see my insurance rates go up simply because drug users are trying to get the unnecessarily high amount of money to buy their drugs? Why must families of non-violent drug users be split apart and, in many cases, put on welfare because their breadwinner is imprisoned for the non-violent possession or usage of illicit drugs? And why must my taxes go up appreciably to support this entire failed enterprise? There must be a better way! And there is!

But first, an honest discussion of this issue is not at all complete without addressing and acknowledging the drug money harm our country has directly inflicted upon the people of the developing world because of our own appetite for illicit drugs. The ultimate irony is that we could "bulldoze" the entire country of Colombia — and even take Peru and Ecuador with it — and those acts would not make the slightest difference in our nation's drug problems. That is because if the demand is here, the demand will be met.

So if the demand is not met by Colombia, Peru, and Ecuador, it will be met by Nigeria, Thailand, and Afghanistan. Or even by California, where marijuana has long been that state's largest cash crop! And as for concerns about violence and other serious harms resulting from our drug policy, in many nations like Colombia and Mexico the drug dealers often outspend and even outgun the police. This directly results in some honest police officers being assassinated, and others giving in to economic coercion and joining forces with the drug dealers. In addition to bloody battles and even running firefights between the police and the drug gangs, right-wing paramilitary fighters have been organized in an effort to fight against many left-wing organizations that are supporting themselves with drug monies. So for years, there have been almost full-scale wars between those groups, accompanied by extortion, mass killings, and even suicide bombings. Then the ultimate irony comes when the winners of these wars almost always take over the lucrative drug trade for themselves.

There are even many truly harmful consequences of our drug policy that we never could have anticipated. For example, some fathers who raise opium poppies in Afghanistan lose their crops as a result of our country's eradication efforts, and most of them have already borrowed money from the drug dealers in reliance upon their eventual sale. So they were increasingly being forced to sell their young daughters to the drug dealers to pay their debts. Afghans disparagingly call these young girls "loan brides," because the fathers give them to the drug dealers as the only way they have to pay their debts.

Of course, we have also had our fair share of drug money harm. I even have a personal story about this. When I was first appointed as a judge, I took the seat of a fairly young man who, for reasons still unknown to me, decided that he no longer wanted to be a judge and resigned. Eight years later, former Judge Alan A. Plaia was convicted in federal court in Hawaii for conspiracy to distribute 220 pounds of cocaine.

I have no reason to believe former Judge Plaia was a bad man; instead, I believe he was simply overcome by the allure of the big and easy money to be made by the sale of illicit drugs. And he is not at all alone. Many people from all walks of life in our country have been convicted of drug money offenses, including twenty-six members of the Los Angeles Sheriff's Office who were convicted for skimming some drug money they had seized. That not only included the officers out in the field, but also the desk sergeant back at headquarters. And without much difficulty we all can find stories in our newspapers virtually every day about similar convictions of people like police commissioners and chiefs of police, judges, mayors, former Justice Department lawyers, FBI agents, border guards, military personnel, airline employees, immigration inspectors and criminal prosecutors, and even a Roman Catholic priest.

A related problem is the material increase in the criminal acts of juvenile gangs throughout our country, which are exacerbated by the fact that the sales of illicit drugs provide the funding for most of those gangs. Not only that, but many of the more sophisticated gangs have begun to extort their drug customers in management positions in government offices, car dealerships, mortgage companies, and others to provide them with access to credit and other personal information of their customers to use for identity theft offenses. As a result of all of this, many young people join the gangs expressly so that they can "be a part of the action," to the extent that most gangs use the sale of illicit drugs as a recruiting tool! So, once again our drug policy is affirmatively fueling anti-social and criminal conduct. And none of these problems are caused by the drugs themselves, they are all caused by the drug money!

Another serious problem was often presented to me while I was on the Abused and Neglected Children's Calendar in Juvenile Court. There would be, for example, a single mother of two children who made a big mistake in that she "hooked up" with the wrong boyfriend. This man would be selling drugs, and the mother would know it, but that is the way the table was set. Then one day, for example, the drug dealer would tell the mother that if she would take a package across town and "give it to Charlie," he would pay her $500. She would basically know that the package contained narcotics, but it would pay half her month's rent and she needed the money. So she would do it, and then get arrested, convicted, and sentenced to about five years in prison. And, to be honest, a sentence of five years for transporting four or five ounces of cocaine in today's system is not an unreasonable sentence.

But ask yourself this question: When the mother is sent to prison what happens to her children? Well, when the mother is confined, she has legally abandoned her children. As a result that case would come to me on the Abused and Neglected Children's calendar. So now I would have in my courtroom the young mother in a jail jumpsuit and handcuffs. And I would tell her the truth, which was that she would not be a functional part of her children's lives for the next five years — and she would start to get tears in her eyes at that realization. Then I would tell her the blunt reality that, unless she either had a close personal friend or family member who was both willing and able to take custody of her children, her children would probably be adopted by somebody else by the time she was released from prison. And then the mother would break down completely — and wouldn't you?

Unfortunately, if that is not enough to get an emotional response from you, I can break you down as a taxpayer. Why? Because, in this example, taxpayers will be spending upwards of $5,000 per month to keep each of these children in a group home until they can be adopted, plus about $70,000 for a year to keep their mother in prison. That means that for the first year, we as taxpayers will be spending about $60,000 per child, times two children, plus the mother's incarceration, for a total cost of about $190,000 to separate a mother from her children! And guess who gets to enforce that program? I do. But at least I did not have to do so quietly.

But there is more because, so far, we have not even discussed other serious and additional unintended consequences that we have suffered as a direct result of our nation's failed policy of Drug

Prohibition. For example, we have lost more of our civil liberties as a result of this policy than anything in our history. In a book I wrote on the failures of Drug Prohibition, I arbitrarily selected 1971, which was the year I graduated from USC Law School, as a cut-off date. Then, by citing only drug cases decided by the United States Supreme Court, I demonstrated how we have lost many of our Fourth Amendment rights, as well as many of our rights under the First, Fifth, and Sixth Amendments as well, solely because of Drug Prohibition. In a similar fashion, we have lost our civil and procedural rights to the government because of asset forfeiture laws in drug cases. And why is no one spreading the alarm? When we lose our precious liberties to the government, we almost never get them back. And all of this has happened because of drug money.

Another consequence of the failure of our national drug policy is seen when people who are suffering from serious pain are unable to obtain sufficient pain relief medication from their doctors. As a result, today there are literally tens of thousands of people in our country who are unnecessarily in great yet treatable pain. This is because the DEA is looking over the shoulders of medical doctors with the express intent of prosecuting any of them who "over-prescribe" addicting pain medication. This rightfully has doctors so paranoid that many of them are actually under-prescribing painkillers to very people who need them.

I refer to this as the "Rush Limbaugh problem." To be honest, I would figuratively love to put this bombastic fellow in jail for lots of reasons, but this is not one of them. If Mr. Limbaugh actually had severe back pain, why should he allegedly have had to acquire pain medication illegally in order for him to alleviate it? All because of our nation's drug policy. You may not be personally aware of this problem yet, but you or least your parents probably will be in the future. Similarly, due to Drug Prohibition, our country's medical community has been virtually forced to stop all research into the physiological reasons for drug addiction and its treatment, as well as the undeniably positive effects of the CBD oil in marijuana or cannabis. As a result, we are only now beginning to discover some promising pharmaceutical treatments for chronic pain and chemical addictions.

But the most far-reaching and ironical unintended consequence is the drug money damage that our current drug policy is doing to our children. When it comes down to it, most people are at least somewhat aware of some of the problems discussed above and realize that what we are doing is not working. But they are willing to continue with the same failed policy, "for all of its defects," in order to keep these dangerous drugs away from our children. However, this policy directly puts our children in harm's way for each of two important reasons.

First, it is actually easier for our young people to obtain marijuana or any other illicit drug, if they want to, than it is for them to get a six-pack of beer. That is what high school and college-age students under the age of twenty-one tell me, and they will tell you the same thing if you ask them. You might say that no one would want to get your thirteen-year-old daughter hooked on cocaine, but you would be wrong. They do want to get her hooked, so that they can make money from her.

Today, no one provides a free sample of Budweiser beer on a high school campus, because they will face real trouble if they were to do such a thing. But free samples of marijuana, ecstasy, and other illicit drugs are made available to our children all the time, even on their school campuses. This brings me to one of the big secrets that our society must learn before we will begin to make progress in this entire area: Prohibition Never Works as Well as Regulation and Control. The reality is that when we prohibit a substance, we give up all of our ability to control it. And when this is done, we concede the entire market to the control of illicit drug dealers — and they do not ask children for identification. As such, the biggest oxymoron in our world of today is the term "Controlled Substances" because, once they are made illegal, all of the controls are turned over to the bad guys! Believe me, it is not at all a pretty picture!

Second, it is really quite easy for an adult drug seller to convince a fourteen or fifteen-year-old boy, or girl, to take a substantial amount of risk almost anywhere for $50 in cash. As a result, drug dealers routinely have as large a supply of these children as they want to act as lookouts, "go-fers," couriers, or anything else. Then, as soon as the child's reliability is established, the drug dealer trusts him or her to sell small amounts of drugs so that both the drug dealer and the children make more money. And, ask yourself, when children sell drugs, who do they logically sell them to? Obviously to their peers, thus recruiting more children to a lifestyle of drug usage and drug selling. I saw this frequently in Juvenile Court and, once again, this is all directly caused by drug money.

At the end of the day, we simply must question ourselves about what our nation's drug policy is doing. Has incarcerating all of these people really made any difference in the availability of the drugs to adults or even to children? Will the potential ruining of the lives of about ninety-five young people who were arrested in April of 2008 at San Diego State University for selling drugs on campus make any positive difference in the availability or use of any of these drugs on that campus, or anywhere else? Are we in better shape today because we have lost many of our constitutional rights because of our War on Drugs? Are narcotics less available to illicit users because medical doctors under-treat the severe pain of many thousands of chronic sufferers? Do we really want to increase the power of organized groups of juvenile and adult criminals here and all around the world? Are there better ways of addressing these critically important issues? And will these other policies better protect our children from the perils and dangers of these mind-altering and sometimes-addicting drugs? I think that if you see what is really happening in the world your answers will be the same as mine.

When it comes down to it, different situations with different people should give rise to different societal responses. Our present policy basically preaches that all illicit drugs are equally dangerous, all use is "bad," and all such drug use should be prohibited. The same approach is taken for adults in the workplace regarding drug testing. In supporting that approach, the Commission on Organized Crime's report in 1986 stated that "a person can no more tolerate a little recreational drug use than he or she can tolerate a little recreational smallpox." This is a naïve and even silly thing to say.

When I talk about these issues publicly, I often acknowledge that most days after work I go home and take a mind-altering and sometimes-addicting substance, that is, I have a glass of wine with dinner. Sometimes I have two. That is to say that I use this mind-altering and sometimes-addicting substance. I also confess that on a few occasions when I was younger, I misused alcohol to the extent that I got sick to my stomach and the next day had a hangover. But I am really careful not to drive after drinking alcohol, and I have never assaulted anyone while under the influence (or at any other time).

If my "drug of choice" were different, and I were brought into the criminal justice system, I would clearly be labeled as a drug addict that needs treatment because I use this substance almost every day. Many people do the same thing. But I believe I am not a problem user and do not need any alcohol treatment whatsoever, but if that were my only hope of escaping a criminal conviction for my drug usage, I would be first in line to sign up. This, of course, would be a waste of public resources.

Otherwise, if people were to go home after work and drink ten martinis and then go to sleep, that certainly would not be a healthy thing to do. In fact, that would be an abuse of the drug of alcohol. And if those people continued that alcohol abuse, even in the face of serious negative consequences in their lives, those people would be considered to be addicted to alcohol. But none of those situations would or should expose them to criminal prosecution unless their actions exposed other people to harm. Then they would be problem users who should be prosecuted. Society can try to help the non-problem substance abusers to be healthier by trying to educate them about the danger of this conduct, and also by making drug treatment available upon demand. But otherwise we will be forced to leave them to their own poor decisions.

The same thing is true concerning other mind-altering and sometimes-dangerous drugs. Different conditions for different people require different responses. The secret is that the drugs do not have to be illegal to hold people accountable for their actions and to coerce the problem users into treatment.

In 1913, Congress looked at the reality of drug use and abuse in our country, and saw that about 1.3 percent of our population was addicted to narcotic drugs. So, "in its wisdom," it passed the Harrison

Narcotic Act, which began taking us down the road to Drug Prohibition. Then, in the early 1970s, during the Nixon Administration, Congress again observed that about 1.3 percent of our population was drug addicted, so it tightened up our laws and began to pursue Drug Prohibition in earnest. Now, after spending more than a trillion dollars on this program, we still notice that about 1.3 percent of our population is drug addicted.

This information will, or at least should, tell us that no matter how tough we are on this issue, until medical science can develop a better way to deal with the problem, about 1.3 percent of our population will always be addicted to these sometimes-dangerous drugs. We can prosecute heavily and send many thousands of drug-addicted people to jail or we can ease back on our prosecutions, and we will still have about a flat-line 1.3 percent of our population addicted to these drugs.

Thus, we should hold people accountable for their actions, and not for what they put into their bodies. Not only is that consistent with our Libertarian philosophy, it actually works. In our society, if one person harms another person the criminal justice system is well equipped to respond. The victim will call the offense to the attention of the authorities, and will cooperate in the crime's investigation and prosecution. But if a willing drug dealer sells an illicit drug to a willing buyer, no one will come forward or even cooperate in the investigation or prosecution of the offense. This forces the criminal justice system to take extraordinary measures to detect, prosecute, and convict any of these people. These measures include surreptitious activities like undercover "sting" operations, wire taps, often unsavory arrangements with paid informants, and encouraging defendants who have already been charged with offenses to "snitch" on other people. Not only are these prosecutions more difficult, they are also much more labor intensive, expensive, unreliable, and physically dangerous for most people involved.

To put this issue in a different perspective, it makes as much sense to me to put that gifted actor Robert Downey, Jr. in jail for his heroin addiction (and he certainly seems to have one), as it would have to put Betty Ford in jail for her alcohol addiction. Nevertheless, if Robert Downey Jr., Betty Ford, or anyone were to drive a motor vehicle impaired by any of these drugs, or do anything else to put other people's safety into jeopardy, bring them to court. If they are problem users, we can then coerce them into drug treatment. Otherwise, what they have is a medical problem. It makes much more sense to me to have medical problems addressed by medical professionals rather than by police officers.

The U.S. Supreme Court has actually acknowledged this distinction in 1962 in Robinson v. California. In that case, Mr. Robinson had been convicted of a California statute that made it a criminal offense to be addicted to the use of narcotics. But Justice Potter Stewart, in writing for the majority, said that making the status of narcotic addiction a criminal offense for which an offender could be prosecuted before he reformed and, upon conviction required that he be imprisoned for at least ninety days, inflicted a "cruel and unusual punishment" upon him.

Unfortunately, over four dissenting opinions, Robinson was ignored in Powell v. Texas, which affirmed a conviction for public drunkenness to alcohol. Justice Abe Fortas in dissent cited the holding of Robinson and said that "even one day in prison would be a cruel and unusual punishment for the 'crime' of having a common cold."

And Justice Fortas was right; Robinson's precedent has been basically forgotten ever since.

Fortunately, under Sundance v. Municipal Court, people in California still cannot be prosecuted for being addicted to alcohol. The California Supreme Court supported the trial court findings of Judge Harry Hupp that if people are unable to stop drinking despite the negative effects it has upon their health and general wellbeing, then the penal system "has no positive effect" in deterring or treating them. Therefore, they could not be arrested unless they would be screened and evaluated by a person who was trained to recognize their medical problems, and their condition monitored at least every hour.

As a trial judge overseeing the prosecution of people addicted to a number of mind-altering and sometimes-addicting drugs other than alcohol, I wonder why the court system, at least in California under the Sundance precedent, has not reached similar findings regarding those other drug-addicted people as well.

Within the last few decades, most of the countries in Western Europe have taken a different approach to the nagging and difficult problems resulting from the presence of mind-altering and sometimes-addicting drugs in their communities. The people in these countries almost universally do not condone drug misuse or abuse any more than we do, but they have adopted the more sophisticated understanding that these drugs, dangerous as they can be, are here to stay. So they have decided to be managers of the problems, instead of simply moralizing about them as a matter of "chemical chastity," or hoping to incarcerate their way out of them. Those countries are doing far better with their efforts than we are. In my view, we can learn from their experiences and more sophisticated approach, and we should change our policies accordingly.

In any policy there are always some winners and some losers. That is true for our policies in education and health care, and it certainly is true in the field of drug policy as well. So ask yourself: Who is winning today with our policy of Drug Prohibition? I have six groups of winners.

The first group that is winning is obviously the big-time drug dealers here and all around the world. They are literally making hundreds of millions of dollars each year (tax free), and they are laughing at us as they pocket this money.

The second group is juvenile youth gangs and other hoodlums whose antisocial and criminal acts are primarily funded by the sale of illicit drugs.

The third group that is winning is the people in government that are being paid large tax dollars to fight against the first two groups. Their bureaucracy, funding, and power continue to increase. In fact, what we have is an amazing partnership of the "good guys" and the "bad guys" because they both have a vested interest in the perpetuation of the status quo. But, may I say strongly here that I do not at all blame law enforcement for the problems we are facing in these areas. They have a dangerous job, and they are doing it far better than we have a right to expect. The failure of Drug Prohibition is no more the fault of today's law enforcement than was the failure of Alcohol Prohibition the fault of people like Elliott Ness. The problem is that our drug policy has failed, not law enforcement.

The fourth group is the politicians who get elected and re-elected by "talking tough" on drugs. Not smart, just tough. But this really is our doing, because if the votes were seen to be in favor of being managers of the problems instead of moralists, politicians would get in front and lead the charge for change. Politicians will always follow where the votes are.

The fifth group is comprised of people in the private sector that make money because of increased crime. That includes people who build prisons and those who staff them. As you probably know, the prison guards' union is the strongest lobbying group in California and most other states today, and these people are certainly winning. Other people in this group are those who sell such things as burglar alarm equipment and security services.

The sixth group that is winning is the terrorists. There will always be radical and extremist people in the world who want to do harm to others who are good and law-abiding. But they will be far less dangerous if their funding is taken away. And, make no mistake, Drug Prohibition is the primary source of funding for all of the terrorists of the world. In fact, our policy of Drug Prohibition is the "Golden Goose" of terrorism.

Who is losing under this policy? Virtually everyone else — particularly our children, as we have shown, as well as the taxpayers. So now that we have discussed this critical issue in some detail, I will end this discussion by giving you four suggestions regarding what we as concerned citizens should do right now.

First, we should institute programs of Needle-Exchange wherever injecting drug-addicted people are found. Second, we should institute drug maintenance programs in every town and city in which there is a need, under the guidance of medical professionals instead of police officers. Furthermore, we should not hide these programs from our children; we should actually take them there. The drug-addicted people will tell our children the truth, which is that they would give anything not to have started down this path. That will be honest education that our children will understand and from which they will learn.

Third, we should institute programs of honest education. Our children easily recognize deception and hypocrisy. Obviously there are some benefits in taking these presently illicit drugs because, if there were not, no one would take them. Of course, there are definite and important risks as well, and our children will make much better decisions if they are exposed to an honest appraisal of both the benefits as well as the risks.

Fourth, we should treat marijuana like alcohol.

There would be six primary results of this change. The first five are demonstratively positive, and then we can discuss the sixth. First, taxpayers would save hundreds of millions of dollars that are now being spent in a futile attempt to eradicate marijuana and prosecute and incarcerate non-violent marijuana users. Clearly, we are not very effective at eradicating the stuff. Second, we could tax it, and generate money. But the third benefit would trump the first two because, as we discussed earlier, this change would result in marijuana actually being less available for our children than it is today. Fourth, we would eliminate the emotional and sometimes tragic problems with the entire medical marijuana issue. And fifth, we could restore the traditionally useful and lucrative hemp industry.

With regard to the sixth result, in order to run more strongly the illicit dealers out of business, the cost of the drug would have to be reduced — in fact, it would probably be required to be cut in half, with taxes included. Therefore, it is fundamental economics that if the demand increases or even remains the same, and the price is lowered, usage would be increased. However, we would soon probably experience the same phenomenon as Holland, and, by "making pot boring," the usage of marijuana would, within a few years, go back to where it is today, or maybe even less.

Throughout my entire involvement in recommending that we change away from our present so-called War on Drugs, there has been no question in my mind that someday we will change our policy. I do not know when, and I do not know to what, but the change certainly will occur, and already has been in some states. And, after these changes do occur, I guarantee that all of us will stand up as one and look at each other in amazement that we could have allowed such a failed and hopeless policy to have been enforced for such a long period of time. So, the sooner you help us to make these changes, the better the entire world will be.

Conclusion

The purpose of this book has been to galvanize discussions about numbers of critical issues facing our country. As I have probably proved on each page, I do not propose to "have all of the answers." But if these pages can promote more full discussions, then that will be gratification enough — because today we are unnecessarily failing in all of the areas discussed.

So please contemplate these suggestions. I truly believe that the Libertarian approaches proposed herein will make us a kinder, more productive and successful society. And if you have comments or suggestions about how these suggestions can be improved, please do not hesitate to contact me through my website, which is www.JudgeJimGray.com. And you can also hear quite a bit more about these issues on my weekly podcast, which has the same title as this book and which you can hear on the Variety Channel at www.VoiceAmerica.com.

In the meantime, best wishes and thank you for your interest in these Libertarian approaches, and Good Luck to us All!

Judge Jim Gray

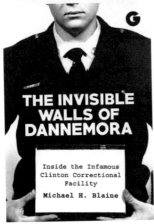